I0477282

Film Actresses

Volume 20

Constance Bennett

Documentary study

Part 1

ISBN-13 : 978-1502972026

ISBN-10 : 1502972026

Copyright©2012-2014 Iacob Adrian

All Rights Reserved.

Dtp
and
graphic design

Iacob Adrian

Copyright©2012-2014 Iacob Adrian
All Rights Reserved.

Author statement

The actors and actresses are the the bricks .

The cast and crew are the plaster .

They stand on the foundation created by
producers and writers and directors .

All these people creates the great palace
of the art of film .

Iacob Adrian - 2013

Copyright©2012-2014 Iacob Adrian
All Rights Reserved.

Hollywood

JUNE

15c in Canada

10 ¢

Visual Study.Iacob Adrian.Copyright©2012-2014.All Rights Reserved.

NRA

JANET GAYNOR
REBELS!

Constance
Bennett

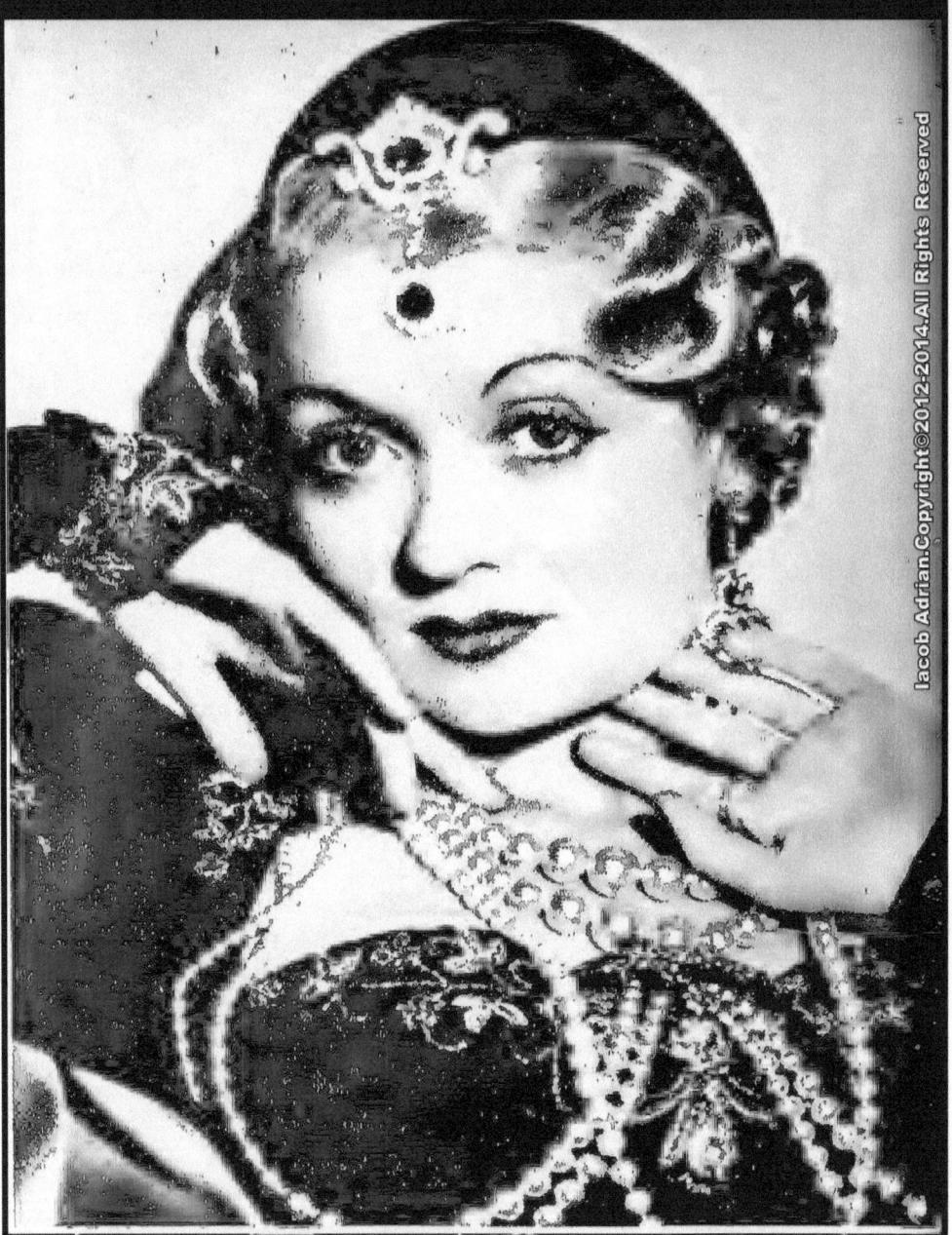

Iacob Adrian.Copyright©2012-2014.All Rights Reserved

Constance

● Elusive, fragile, ethereal beauty cunningly combined with the compelling charm of the woman of the world! With these elaborate trappings of pearls, jewels and gaudy whatnots, Constance Bennett will be seen in *The Affairs of Cellini*, formerly *The Firebrand*, in which Fredric March also stars

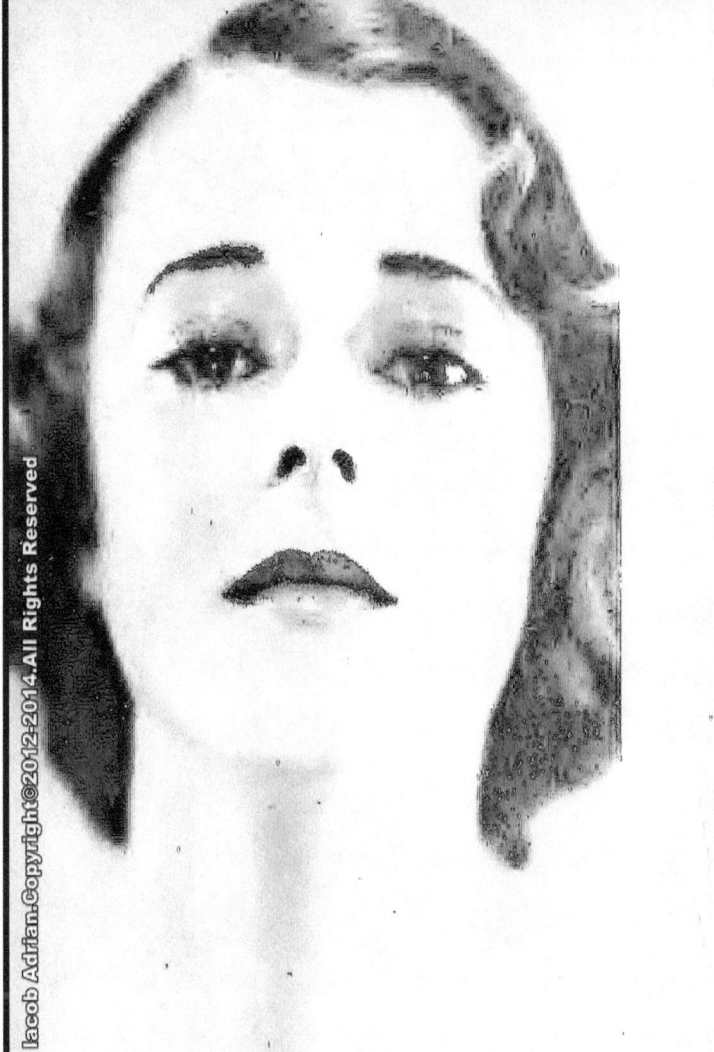

Iacob Adrian.Copyright©2012-2014.All Rights Reserved

Heather Angel

-Jack Freulich

● Speaking of Angels, Heather is a living demonstration of a romantic young man's most cherished dream come true. Big things are planned for Heather at Universal, where she recently assumed an attractive contract, the first of which will be her appearance in *Romance in the Rain*

Constance Bennett

● If it isn't what she is doing it is what she is wearing that makes Connie Bennett the cynosure of all eyes at all times. You'll have a sample of both in *The Green Hat*, the new talkie version of the famous Michael Arlen novel, in which she wears this stunning frock of blister crêpe

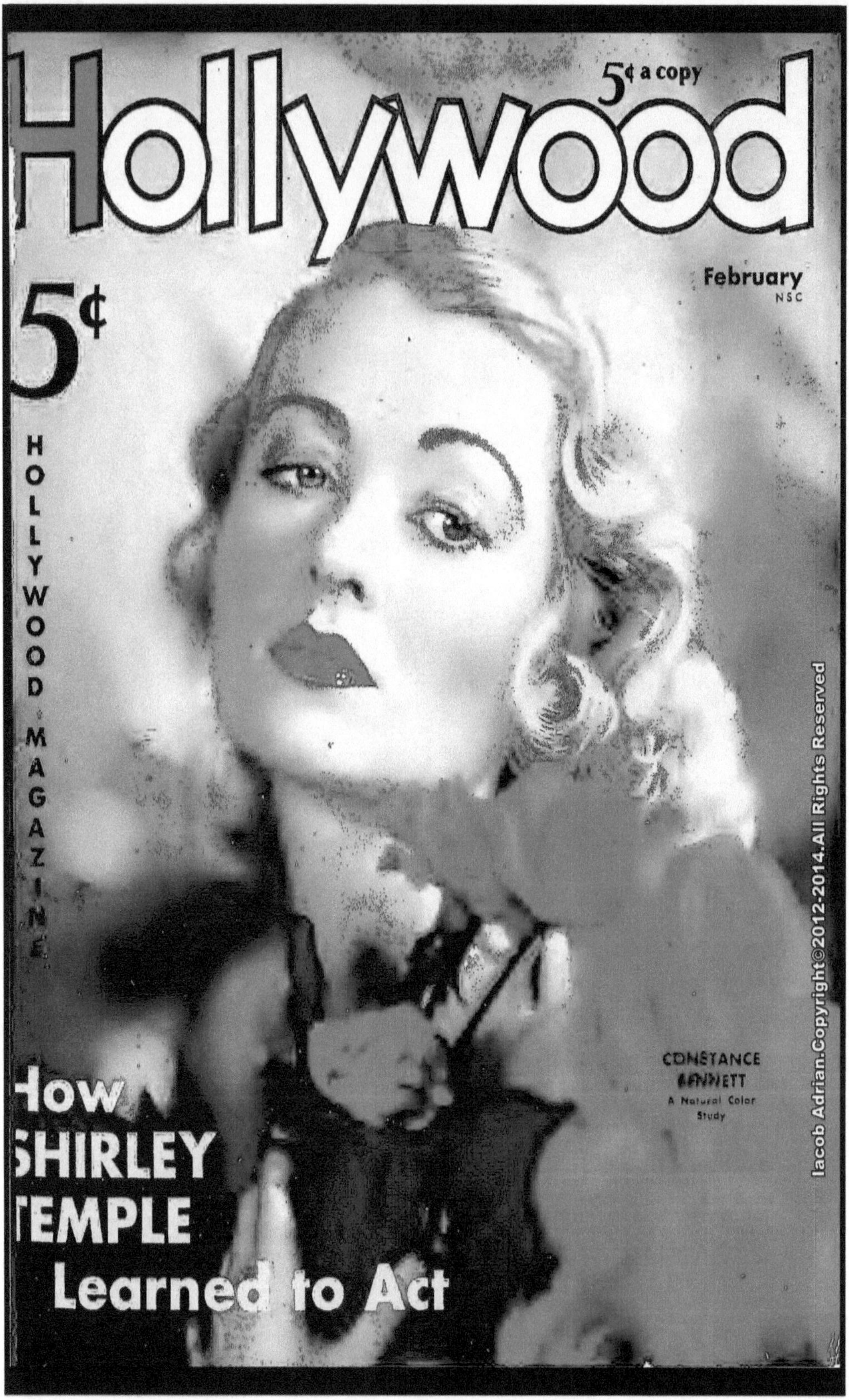

Hollywood

5¢ a copy

February
NSC

5¢

HOLLYWOOD MAGAZINE

Iacob Adrian.Copyright©2012-2014.All Rights Reserved

CONSTANCE
BENNETT
A Natural Color
Study

How
SHIRLEY
TEMPLE
Learned to Act

Star Styles

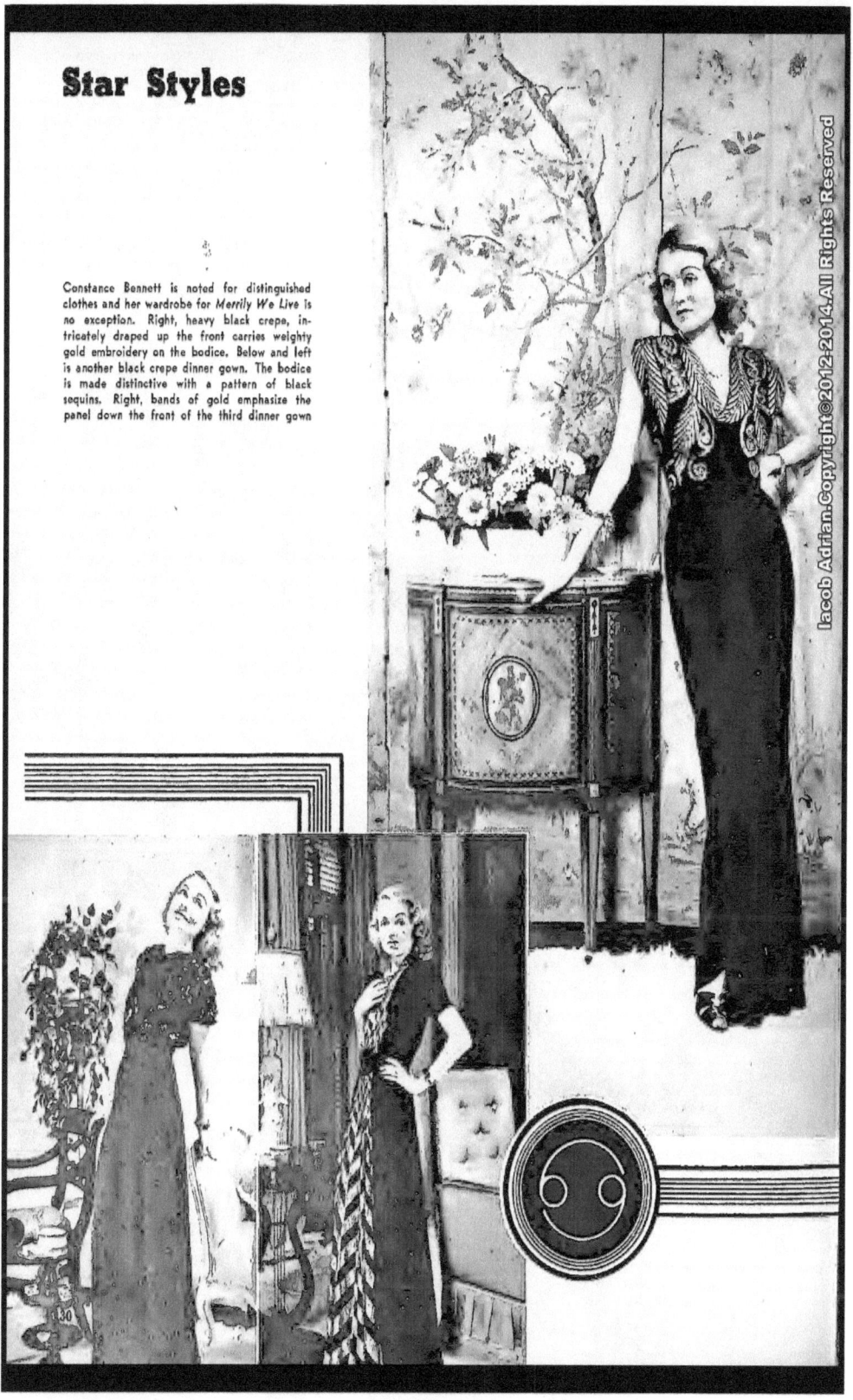

Constance Bennett is noted for distinguished clothes and her wardrobe for *Merrily We Live* is no exception. Right, heavy black crepe, intricately draped up the front carries weighty gold embroidery on the bodice. Below and left is another black crepe dinner gown. The bodice is made distinctive with a pattern of black sequins. Right, bands of gold emphasize the panel down the front of the third dinner gown

Iacob Adrian.Copyright©2012-2014.All Rights Reserved

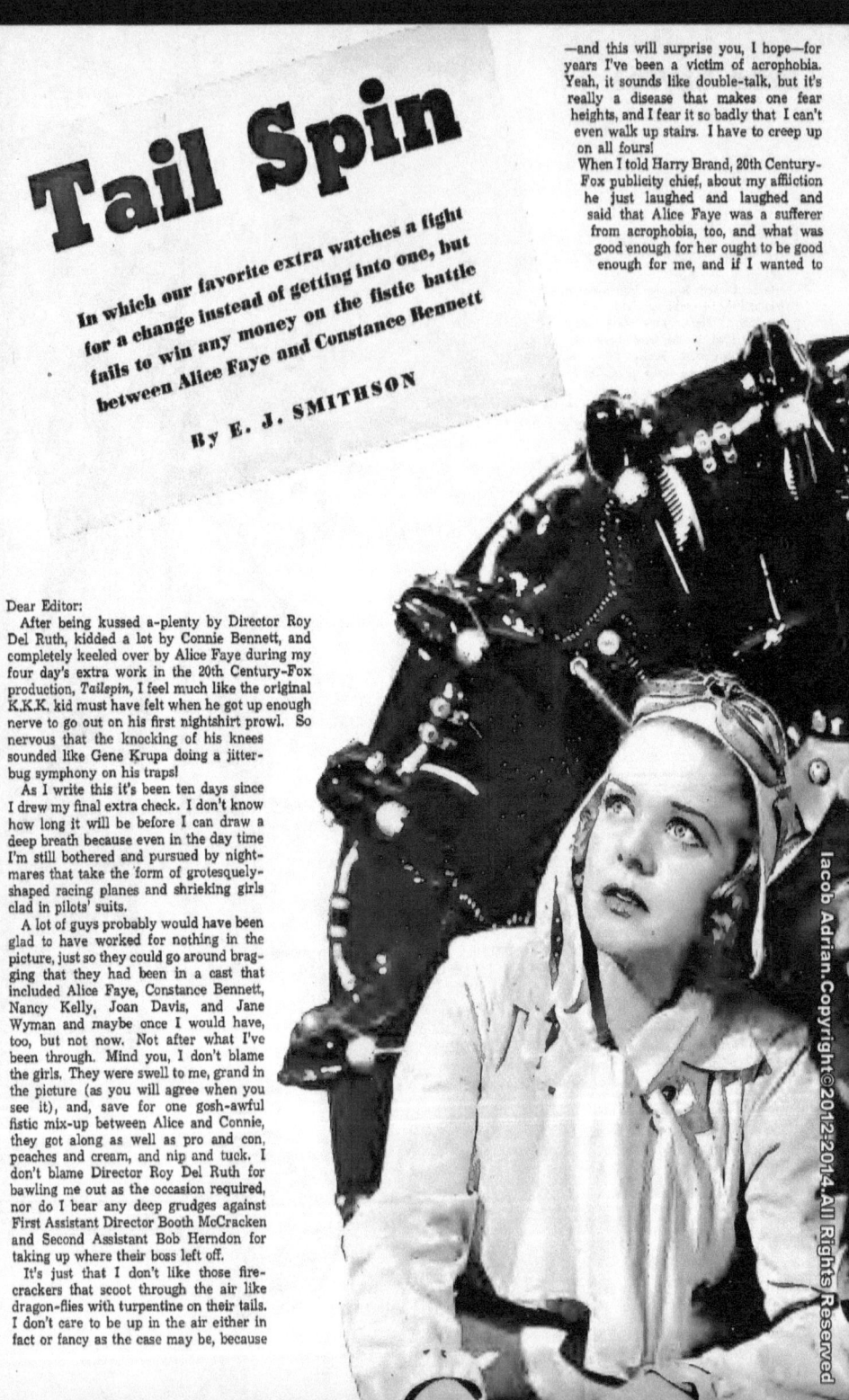

Tail Spin

In which our favorite extra watches a fight for a change instead of getting into one, but fails to win any money on the fistic battle between Alice Faye and Constance Bennett

By E. J. SMITHSON

—and this will surprise you, I hope—for years I've been a victim of acrophobia. Yeah, it sounds like double-talk, but it's really a disease that makes one fear heights, and I fear it so badly that I can't even walk up stairs. I have to creep up on all fours!

When I told Harry Brand, 20th Century-Fox publicity chief, about my affliction he just laughed and laughed and said that Alice Faye was a sufferer from acrophobia, too, and what was good enough for her ought to be good enough for me, and if I wanted to

Dear Editor:

After being kussed a-plenty by Director Roy Del Ruth, kidded a lot by Connie Bennett, and completely keeled over by Alice Faye during my four day's extra work in the 20th Century-Fox production, *Tailspin*, I feel much like the original K.K.K. kid must have felt when he got up enough nerve to go out on his first nightshirt prowl. So nervous that the knocking of his knees sounded like Gene Krupa doing a jitter-bug symphony on his traps!

As I write this it's been ten days since I drew my final extra check. I don't know how long it will be before I can draw a deep breath because even in the day time I'm still bothered and pursued by night-mares that take the form of grotesquely-shaped racing planes and shrieking girls clad in pilots' suits.

A lot of guys probably would have been glad to have worked for nothing in the picture, just so they could go around brag-ging that they had been in a cast that included Alice Faye, Constance Bennett, Nancy Kelly, Joan Davis, and Jane Wyman and maybe once I would have, too, but not now. Not after what I've been through. Mind you, I don't blame the girls. They were swell to me, grand in the picture (as you will agree when you see it), and, save for one gosh-awful fistic mix-up between Alice and Connie, they got along as well as pro and con, peaches and cream, and nip and tuck. I don't blame Director Roy Del Ruth for bawling me out as the occasion required, nor do I bear any deep grudges against First Assistant Director Booth McCracken and Second Assistant Bob Herndon for taking up where their boss left off.

It's just that I don't like those fire-crackers that scoot through the air like dragon-flies with turpentine on their tails. I don't care to be up in the air either in fact or fancy as the case may be, because

Iacob Adrian. Copyright©2012-2014. All Rights Reserved

knock the stuffing out of a Thanksgiving turkey I'd better go over to the casting office and sign up. Well, we actors have to eat despite stories to the contrary, and so I went over to casting as Harry ordered. If Alice Faye could stand it, so could I. And that's where I made my first mistake.

■ The first thing that happened to me once we were on location came in the shape of an invitation from Paul Mantz and Marion McKeen, two famous pilots in the National Air Races, for a short ride "upstairs." Just to get the feel of the air, they said without cracking a smile. Ever been in a ship that coasts along at a trifling 200 miles per hour? Ever come down in one? Honest, after that experience I'm as gabby about it as a woman who loves to talk about her operation!

Well, after I got the "feel" of the ground again I stayed there and earned my Turkey Day money as grease-monkey No. 2. Charlie Farrell was grease-monkey No. 1 and he's just as grand a guy as he used to be "way back when" he was tops among the stars. During the course of the picture it's Charlie, playing a good-natured, happy-go-lucky mechanic, who helps Alice Faye win the women's speed classic at the National Air Races held in Cleveland. It turned out that Charlie used to fly a crate during the days when he and Janet Gaynor were packing 'em in at the box-office. Not only that, but he was taught to fly by none other than Marion McKeen, who is in this picture as technical advisor.

Tail Spin, by the way, is Farrell's second picture on his home lot since his return to American pictures. His first one was with Shirley Temple in *Just Around the Corner* and in that one he showed that the passing years had neither dimmed nor diminished his "pull" before the camera.

Another thing about *Tail Spin* that Charlie liked is the fact that it re-united him with Ruth Clifford. It is the first time in more than a decade that they have worked together. Way back in 1927, Miss Clifford, a star of the first magnitude at that time, was cast for the major feminine role in *The Love Hour*. A young newcomer, as unknown as a man on Mars, was assigned as her leading man. You're right, it was Charlie Farrell. Both went their separate ways after that picture with Farrell climbing to the top and with Miss Clifford dropping out of film work. Their paths did not cross again until they both found themselves in *Tail Spin*.

■ My second day in *Tail Spin* was even more dramatic than the first, although it didn't call for any histrionic effort on my part. Day No. 2 was set aside for the shooting of Nancy Kelly's death—a 6,000-celluloid power dive in a bullet-like racing ship.

"I have never before died on the screen," the wide-eyed Irish lassie explained to us before the shooting began, "so this is an experience toward which I am looking forward with a good deal of anticipation! I think I'll enjoy every moment of it." Quite a girl, this

Alice Faye, Constance Bennett and the sky-rocketing newcomer, Nancy Kelly, carry the leading roles in the film about feminine air-racers, *Tail Spin*

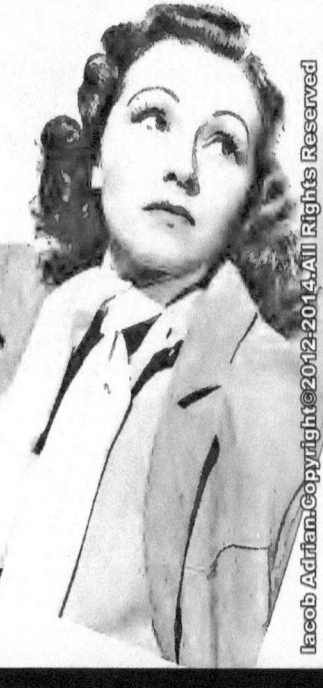

Iacob Adrian Copyright©2012-2014 All Rights Reserved

Tail Spin

By E. J. SMITHSON

In which our favorite extra watches a fight instead of getting into the fiste battle for a chance to win any money and Constance Bennett falls to win any money between Alice Faye and Constance Bennett.

Dear Editor:

After being kissed o-plenty by Director Roy Del Ruth, kidded o-lot by Constance Bennett, and coolly regarded by Alice Faye during my four day's extra work in the 20th Century-Fox production, Tailspin, I feel much like the original K.K.K. kid must have felt when he got up enough nerve to go out on his first nightclub prowl. So nervous that I let the bartender do my jitterbug symphony on his impel.

As I write this it's been ten days since I drew my final extra check. I don't know how long it will be before I can draw a deep breath before I can again see what I've been through during my picture pursued by nightmares that take the form of grotesquely-shaped racing planes and shrieking girls clad in pilots' suits.

A lot of guys probably would have been glad to have worked for weeks with the picture, just as they would not mind being that they had been in a cast that included Alice Faye, Constance Bennett, Nancy Kelly, Joan Davis, and Jane Wyman, and maybe once I would have, too, but not now. Not for what I've been through. Don't blame me, I don't blame the picture (as you will agree when you see it), and save for one gosh-awful fistic mix-up between Alice and Connie, they got along fine, and nip and tuck. I don't blame Director Roy Del Ruth for bawling me out on the occasion required, nor do I blame any deep grudge against First Assistant Director Booth Mc Cracken and sadistic assistant Bob Herndon for taking up where their boss left off.

It's just that I don't like those fire-crackers that scoot through the air like dragon-flies with turpentine on their tails. I don't care to go up in the air so fast or fancy as the case may be, because

and this will surprise you, I hope—for years I've been a victim of acrophobia. Yeah, it sounds like double-talk, but it's really a disease that makes one fear heights, and walking up stairs I have to creep up on all fours!

When I told Harry Brand, 20th Century-Fox publicity chief, about my affliction he just laughed and laughed and said he'd cure me. Acrophobia, too, and what was from acrophobia, too, and what was good enough for her ought to be good enough for me, and if I wanted to knock the stuffing out of a Thanksgiving turkey I'd better go over to the casting office and sign up. Well, we actors have to eat despite stories to the contrary, so I did. Ever come down in one? Honest, after that experience I'm as pale about it as a woman who loves to talk about her first mink.

Well, after I got the "feel" of the ground again I stayed there and earned my Turkey Day money as grease-monkey No. 2. Charlie Farrell was grease-monkey No. 1. Say, but he's grand a guy as he was to be "back for," for he was tops among the stars. Now it's Charlie, playing a good-natured, happy-go-lucky mechanic, who helps Alice Faye win the women's speed classic at the National Air Races held in Cleveland. It turned out that Charlie used to fly a crate during the days when he was taught to fly by none other than Marion McKeen, who is his technical advisor.

■ The first thing that happened to me in the shape of an invitation from Paul and Marion McKeen, two famous pilots in the National Air Races, for a short ride

"quickin," just to get the feel of the air, they said while cracking a smile. Ever been in ship that cracking a smile. Ever 300 miles per hour?

Tail Spin, by the way, is Farrell's second picture on his

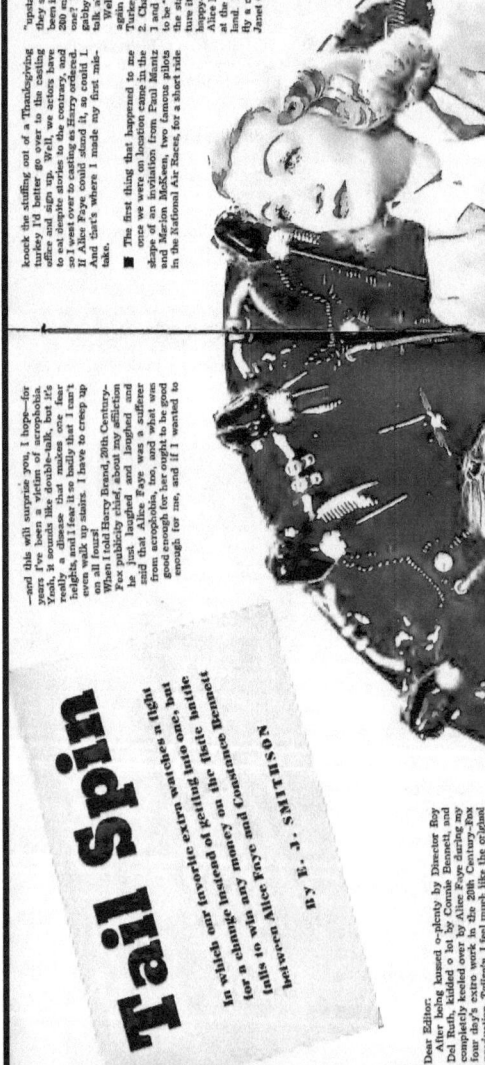

home lot since his return to American pictures. His first one was with Shirley Temple in Just Around the Corner and he learned that the passing years had neither dimmed nor diminished his "pull" before the camera.

Another thing about Tail Spin that Charlie liked is the fact that it re-united him with Ruth Clifford. It is the first time in seventeen years that they have worked together. Way back in 1927, Miss Clifford, a star of the first magnitude at that time, was cast for the major feminine role in The Love Hour. A young newcomer, a unknown man on Mars, was assigned as her leading man, so we're right, it was Charlie Farrell. Both went their separate ways after that picture with Farrell climbing to the top and with Miss Clifford dropping out of film work. Their paths did not cross again until they both found themselves in Tail Spin.

■ My second day in Tail Spin was even more dramatic than the first, although it didn't call for any historionic effort on my part. Dull for any historionic effort on the shooting of Nancy Kelly's death—a 6,000-celluloid power dive in a bullet-like racing ship.

"I have never before died on the screen," the pretty Miss Kelly explained to us before the shooting began. "So it is an experience toward which I am looking forward with a good deal of anticipation. I think I'll enjoy every moment of it." Quite a girl, this [Continued on page 63]

Alice Faye, Constance Bennett and the appealing newcomer, Nancy Kelly, carry the leading roles in the film about heroines the air-aces, Tail Spin.

Visual Study.Iacob Adrian.Copyright©2012-2014.All Rights Reserved.

Iacob Adrian Copyright ©2012-2014 All Rights Reserved

"My contract has two years to go," says Connie, "and anything may happen in that time."

CONNIE BENNETT is variously reported as having no sense of humor, being up-stage, temperamental and hard to handle, but the directors and camera crew on her sets declare her a good trouper and a good scout ... and to prove she has a sense of humor and that it works, listen to this:

She was doing a scene in which she had to run up and down a flight of stairs.

Suddenly, after several rehearsals, the director called, "Hold it! Cameras and recorder reloading."

Connie Bennett's sense of humor . . . Connie's charities . . . Connie and her retirement . . .

Connie was completely out of breath and gratefully dropped into the nearest chair, puffing mightily.

"O.K. Cameras and recorder reloaded," called the assistant director.

But Connie sang out lustily, "Hold it! Bennett still reloading!" and she puffed a few more minutes before the scene was resumed.

HOLLYWOOD loves to keep the Constance Bennett-Gloria Swanson feud alive.

The latest story going the rounds is that on a little side street in Culver City, near the studio where the two stars once worked, is a corner grocery store labeled "Bennett's Best Foods." On the opposite corner is a delicatessen defiantly

Constance Bennett Items

announcing "Swanson's Delicatessen."

These two little stores carry on a price war by means of red-lettered placards and manage to keep up quite a spirited rivalry.

The natives say that it was during all the bitter rivalry between their namesakes that these merchants began to cut prices on each other. At first they carried it on in a spirit of fun, but as time has passed they have taken it seriously and are now bitter enemies!

QUITE a stir was caused when the English press began to call Constance Bennett on the telephone to know just when she intended going to England to live. She had denied the rumors emphatically but no one seemed to believe her.

After finishing her picture for Warners and one more for Radio, she and the Marquis will trek to France for a three-month's rest—if they haven't gone already. Connie plans a gay autumn on the Riviera and then a month in Paris where she keeps an apartment

all the year around in readiness for her annual vacation.

Connie has said, here and there, that when her contract is finished with R.-K.-O. she will retire, at least for a while, and live abroad. But Connie is a woman, after all, and apt to change her mind several dozen times within the next two years, until her contract expires.

Joel McCrea is always seeking new ways of amusing himself and others. One day he conceived the idea of taking down all the photographs of Constance Bennett's personal friends which decorate her dressing room and substituting photographs of would-be suitors found in her fan mail.

He hung up the photograph of a long-jawed sheeprancher where the Marquis' photo had hung, a bushy-browed brewer from Milwaukee where his own likeness had swung in state, a dainty wisp of a thing from London in the place of sister Joan, and several others. All had written under their smiling countenances, "To My Dream Girl" or "To My

Inspiration." Connie was amused and delighted when she saw the substitutions and is now making a collection of fan photographs.

CONNIE tells this one on herself. She had a new burglar alarm installed in her house because a suspicious looking character had been seen prowling about.

The first night of the installation, Connie forgot to touch the little switch to release the alarm when she opened her bedroom window. A piercing bell instantly clanged through the house.

Connie and the Marquis tried frantically to stop the alarm. It rang for fully fifteen minutes—"loud enough to wake the dead," said Connie . . . but the chauffeur, the gardener and the butler, whom the bell was supposed to send scurrying, never let out a peep!

Finally, just as they had managed to still the shrill screams of the bell, a sleepy maid appeared at her door.

Rubbing her eyes, the woman timidly inquired: "Did you ring, madam?"

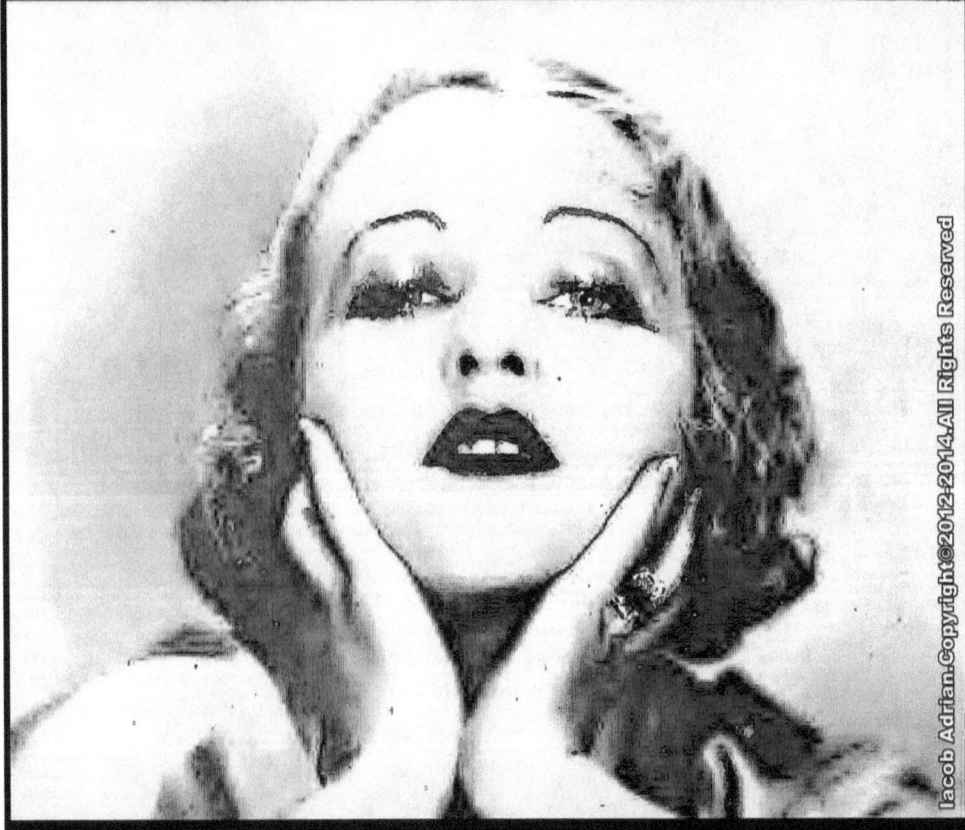

Iacob Adrian Copyright ©2012-2014 All Rights Reserved

Coiffures for Constance

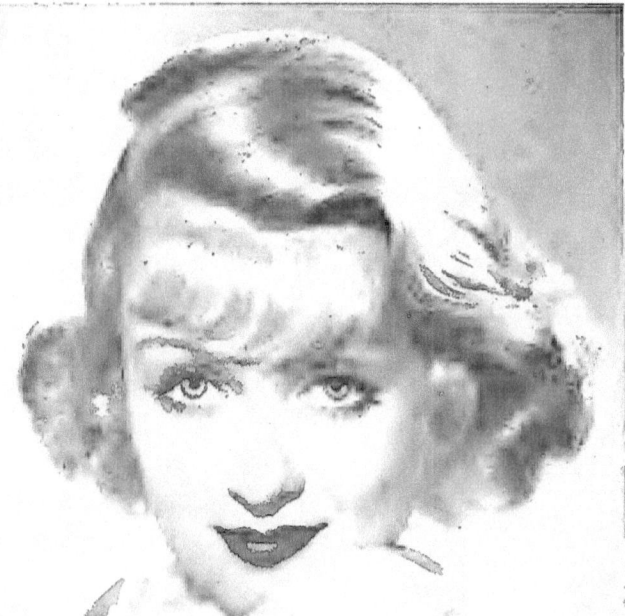

Iacob Adrian.Copyright©2012-2014.All Rights Reserved

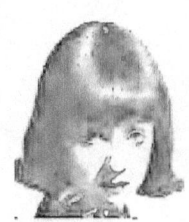

Not even the hairdresser advises Miss Bennett how to arrange her hair and it is her opinion that every girl is her own best critic

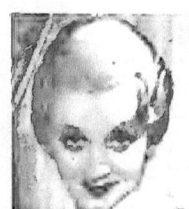

SHOULD a girl vary the arrangement of her hair to suit the occasion?

To this question the truly dress-conscious New Yorker or Parisienne would usually answer, "Emphatically, yes." But Constance Bennett says, "Certainly not."

"An arrangement that would be appropriate for the opera would be out of place on the golf links," says the well dressed American who is not an actress. And the clothes-wise Parisienne considers the line of her costume, the smartly tailored trotteur, or the simple but elegant evening gown before giving directions to her hairdresser. But Constance Bennett says, "One's hair should be dressed in the most becoming fashion regardless of the occasion." And perhaps Constance is right.

This does not mean, however, that Miss Bennett has only one hair arrangement. She has learned the trick of doing her hair in a dozen ways that are all supremely becoming. And in "Moulin Rouge" she even hid her lovely golden tresses under a transforming straight black wig.

Is a girl the best judge of how to arrange her own hair, or should she follow the suggestions of others? To this question Miss Bennett answered, "If she knows her type she should be the best judge. If not she should make a really serious study of her features and then arrange her hair accordingly."

Does Miss Bennett get the hairdresser to make suggestions? No. Does a director or anybody else ever make suggestions? No. Miss Bennett knows her own type better than anyone else, and needs no assistance. And it is her own personal opinion that any girl, whether or not she is gifted with introspection or exceptional self understanding, should decide for herself what hair arrangements are most becoming and therefore most desirable.

"The care of the hair should be of the utmost importance to all women." she said, "regardless of their profession, for hair has been and always will be woman's crowning glory. But no matter how naturally lovely your hair may be, how fine and soft and glossy, it won't take care of itself. Ordinary hair, if well cared for, is more attractive than the most beautiful hair in the world left to its own devices."

Miss Bennett spends an hour at least in arranging her hair before the first scene of the day is photographed, and between scenes time enough to match it up with the preceding scene.

While Constance Bennett and the other leading screen actresses undoubtedly do settle the important question of hair arrangement for themselves. skilled barbers and hairdressers

Coiffures for
Constance

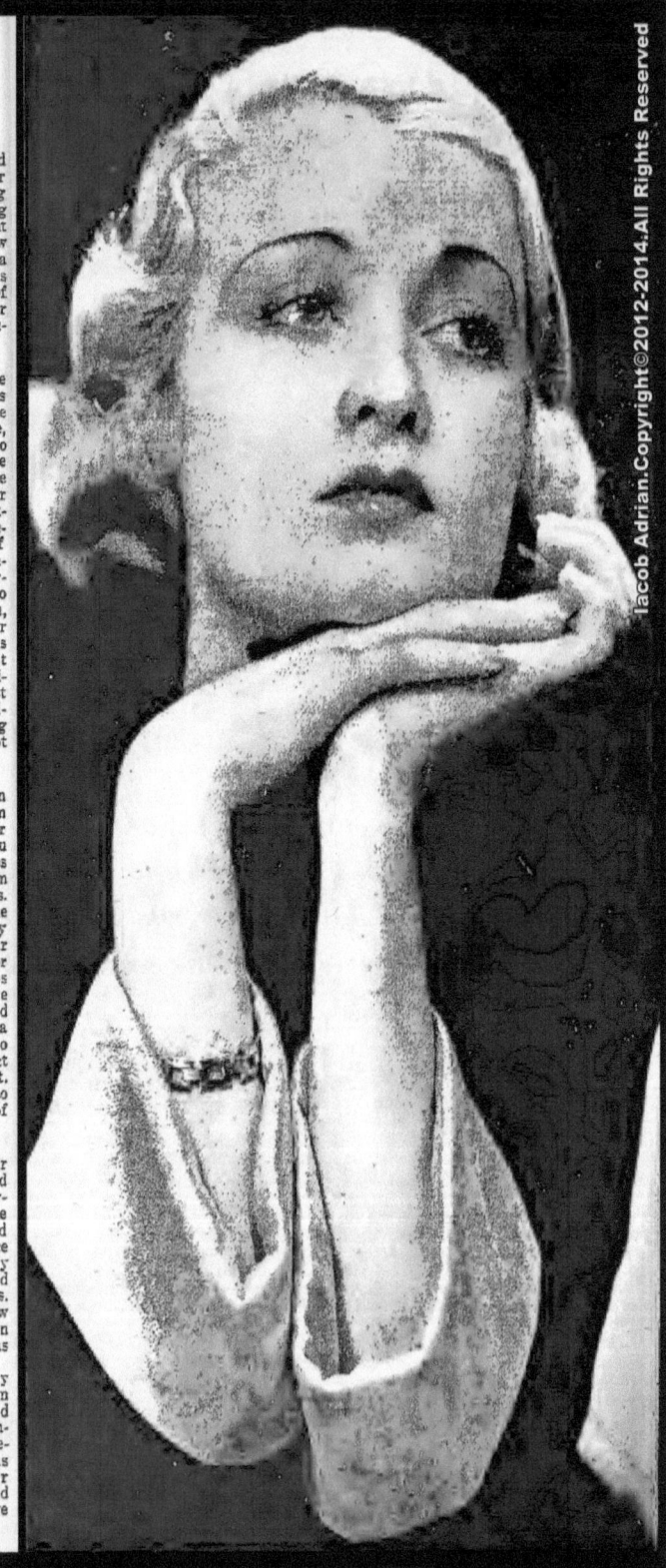

play a big part in giving Hollywood a preeminent position in this matter of hair arrangement. It is one thing to know that a certain type of bang will add a note of infinite bewitchment to the face and another thing to know how to achieve that type of bang by a few deft clips of the scissors. It is one thing to appreciate the charm of softly curling ear locks, and another thing to know by what expert manipulation they can be effected.

ACTUALLY the methods and the preparations used by Hollywood's hairdressers are no different from those used by successful hairdressers here, there and everywhere. There are no secret formulas or applications. The difference between the tactics of the Hollywood coiffeurs and those of other coiffeurs is one that can be easily explained by Hollywood's own requirements. If your interest is one of smartness, of keeping up with the fashions, then when you go to the hairdresser you will naturally ask him to arrange your hair in the latest fashion, a style that will be precisely right for that new hat copied after a Paris model. If you are an actress who must register her individuality on the sensitive film of a camera, then the most important thing is to choose a headdress that is above all else becoming and individual. Mere smartness is not enough.

ONE thing that may strike you on your first visit to Hollywood from New York, Chicago or Paris is that hair is cut longer there than elsewhere. You have heard of the new sleeker coiffures from Paris, and you have seen them successfully worn in American cities. You are surprised when you see the best Hollywood barbers more chary with the scissors. But that your Hollywood barber easily accounts for when he reminds you that an actress never knows precisely what role she may be called upon to play next and that it is very much simpler to give a sleek contour to hair that is a trifle too long than to give a soft, girlish effect to hair that has been cropped too short.

So we may give blame or credit to Hollywood for the continued vogue of the longer bob.

OTHER present-day fashions in hair dressing may undoubtedly be laid at Hollywood's door. The most important of these is the present insistence on glossiness and sheen. Fuzziness and roughness of the hair that might once have been tolerated show up glaringly on the screen. You may have noticed this yourself in your own photographs. Hair that will stand up under this new requirement must be free from broken ends, it must be smooth and lustrous and soft.

If you could compare the beautifully kept hair of the modern young woman of today with the frizzed and scorched and ratted hair of the girl of the pompadour age, you would begin to appreciate the vast improvement that has taken place in hair treatment, hair preparations and waving methods. And if you stop to think you will give motion pictures a share of the credit.

Iacob Adrian.Copyright©2012-2014.All Rights Reserved

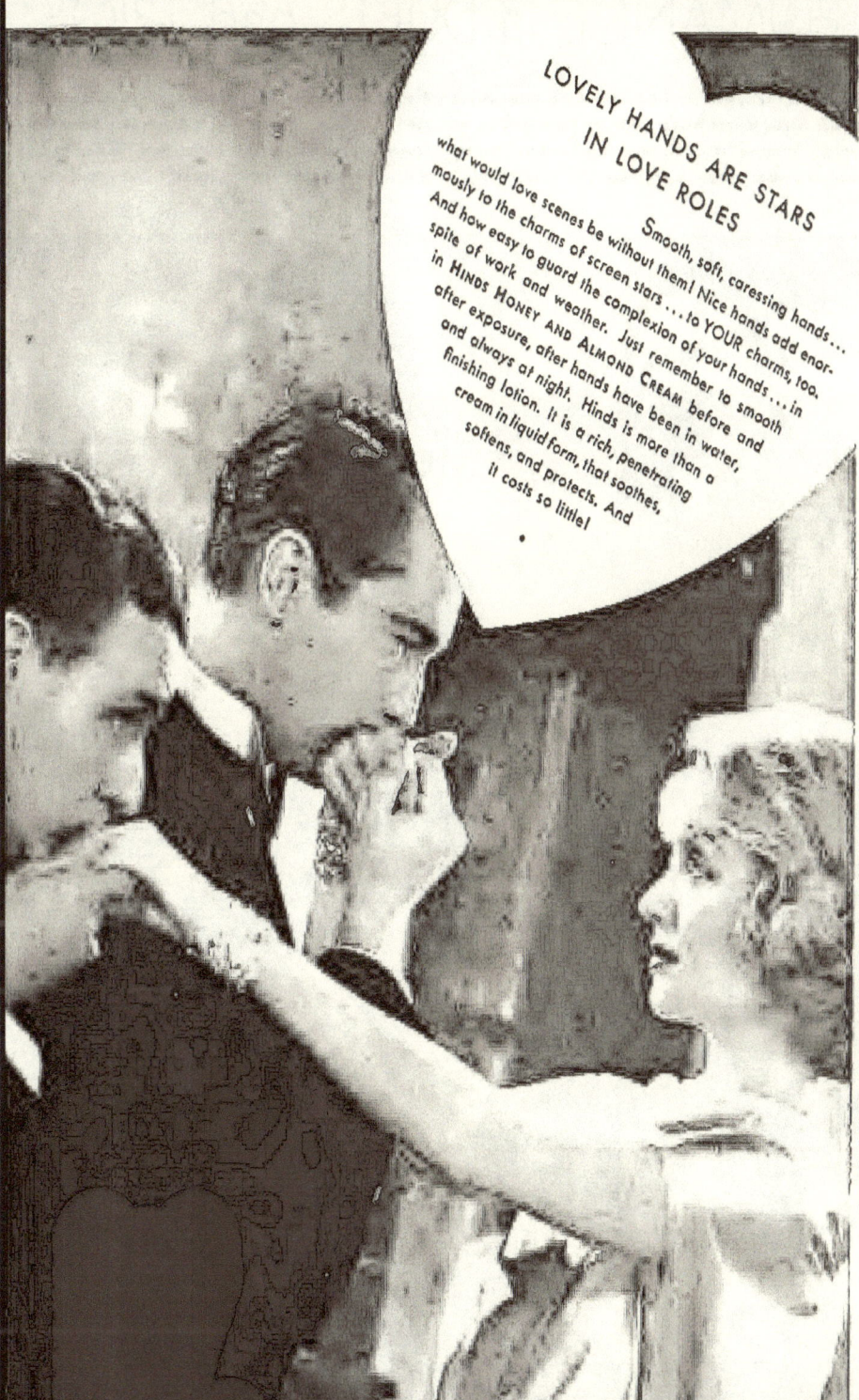

LOVELY HANDS ARE STARS
IN LOVE ROLES

Smooth, soft, caressing hands...
what would love scenes be without them! Nice hands add enor-
mously to the charms of screen stars...to YOUR charms, too.
And how easy to guard the complexion of your hands...in
spite of work and weather. Just remember to smooth
in HINDS HONEY AND ALMOND CREAM before and
after exposure, after hands have been in water,
and always at night. Hinds is more than a
finishing lotion. It is a rich, penetrating
cream in liquid form, that soothes,
softens, and protects. And
it costs so little!

Iacob Adrian.Copyright©2012-2014.All Rights Reserved

ROMANCE in DUETS and TRIOS

For instance, looking down the left-hand border of this page, you see Kay Francis, Warren William and George Brent, in "Living on Velvet." Genevieve Tobin, Gene Raymond and Barbara Stanwyck constitute another triangle, in the swank "The Woman in Red." And Jack Holt, Florence Rice and Edmund Lowe go to make up still another, in "The Best Man Wins." Then, the romantic duos—Gary Cooper and Anna Sten, in "The Wedding Night"; and, in the large photo, Clark Gable and Constance Bennett, in "After Office Hours."

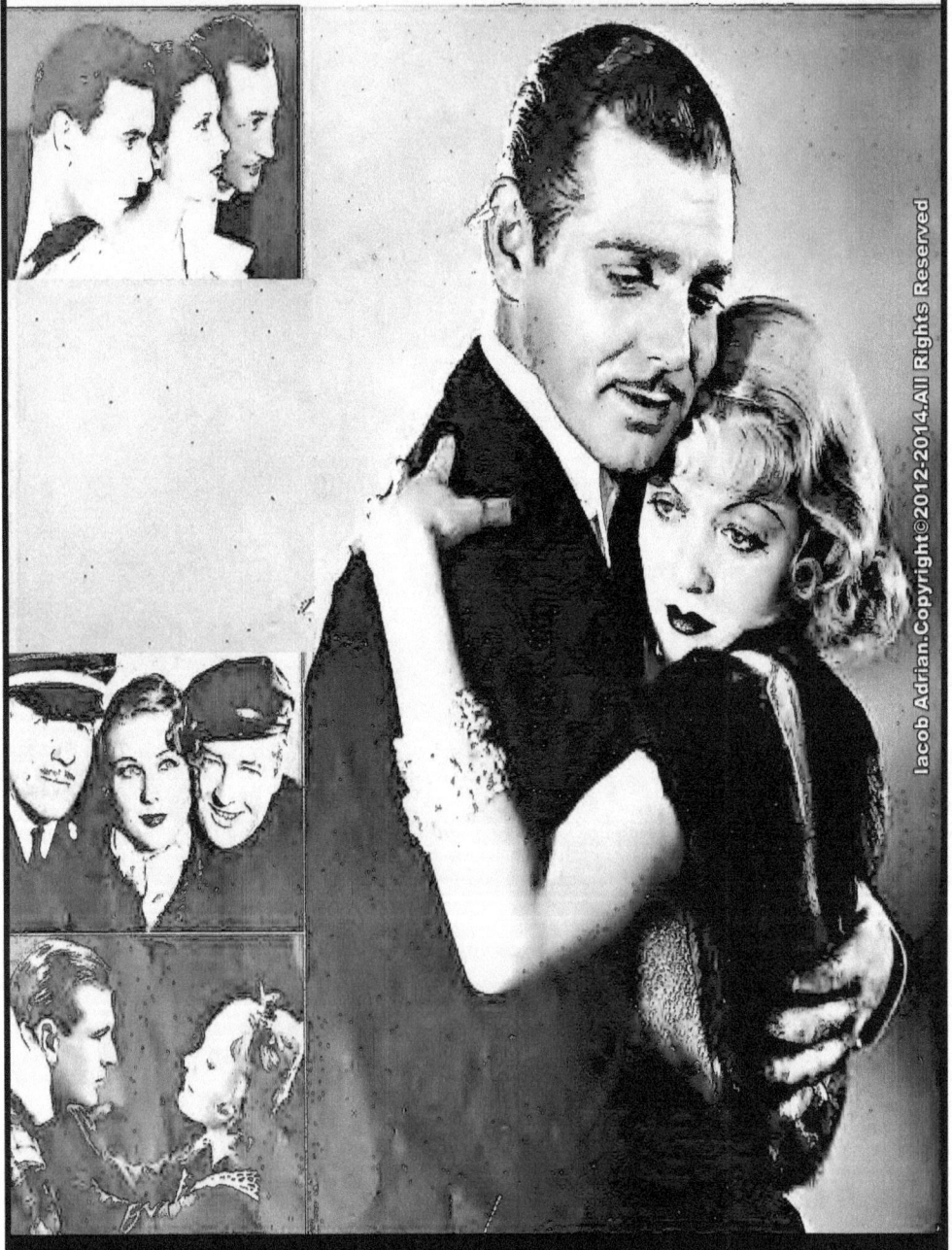

Iacob Adrian.Copyright©2012-2014.All Rights Reserved

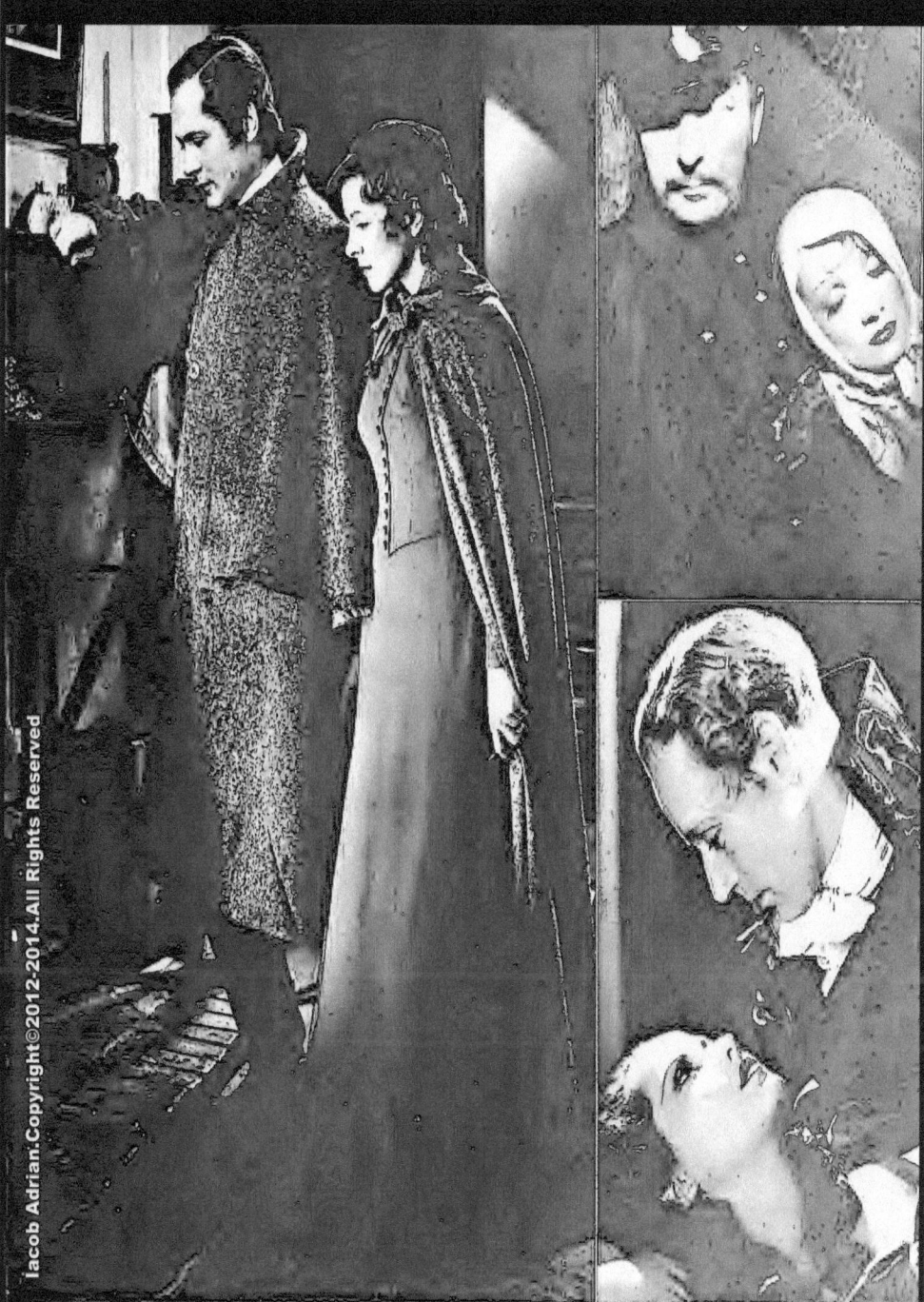

Iacob Adrian.Copyright©2012-2014.All Rights Reserved

Movies comb the world for plots and stories to bring you Romance. And on this page are still other examples of the relentless search. From Great Britain comes the story of "Vanessa," bringing you Robert Montgomery and Helen Hayes as lovers. Spain furnishes the background of "Caprice Espagnole"(right, above) with Lionel Atwill and the provocative Marlene Dietrich. North to Britain, again, goes "The Scarlet Pimpernel," with Merle Oberon and the gallant Leslie Howard. In what far lands shall we find ourselves next month?

A GIRL AND A MAN—OR TWO!—AND THE CAMERAS GRIND ON

CONSTANCE should have been A BOY

BY HER SISTER
JOAN BENNETT

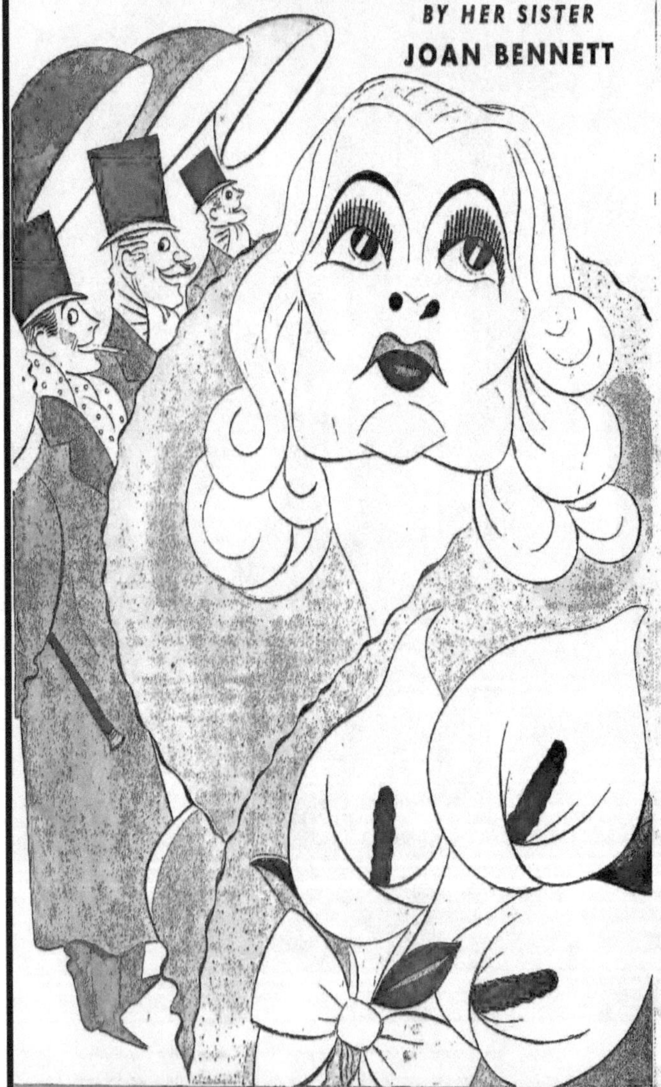

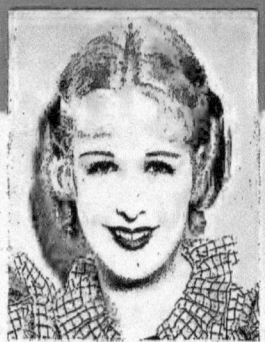

SHE should have been born a boy; for, had such been the case, those very traits of character—that aggressiveness, that daring, that independence, that decisiveness—which have earned her frequent criticism, would have won her unstinted admiration.

Connie is one of the few completely honest women I have known. She says what she thinks, does what she likes—and, man-fashion, takes the consequences of any mistake she may make without a whine. I never have known her to trade on the "privileges" of her sex.

I can readily understand why some people persistently misjudge and resent, or even dislike her. Her cardinal sin lies in the fact that she does not conform to the conventional mould. Furthermore, she is superbly sure of herself, exasperating in her self-confidence. She is, at times, very intolerant. She is sometimes inclined to be overbearing. Having reached a decision, she is prompt to translate it into action, and seldom does she have the patience to explain or defend her motives.

Let the action be its own justification—that, always, has been Connie's way.

Because of the difference in our ages and because of the still wider difference in our temperaments, there has never been between Constance and myself that close companionship which one might expect to find between sisters. Yet we have always been loyal to each other, and, possibly because all members of "that Bennett clan" share certain fundamental traits, we have understood one another remarkably well.

Frankly, I always have stood somewhat in awe of Constance. She always has been the dominant, older sister. She always has told me what to do—and I usually have accepted her counsel, for experience has taught me that she is almost always right.

I have stood in awe of her mental strength and her abilities, not of the fact that she happens to be the elder. She was born to dominate. The effort to rule the lives of those whom she loves is as natural a gesture to her as breathing.

I have stood in awe of the aura of glamour which always has hovered around her. That glamour does not depend on her stardom, or her wealth, or her social position. It is a part of her, a radiation from her personality. It is something that defies exact analysis. To a certain degree, I suppose, it is a by-product of her innate poise and assurance.

Even as a school girl, she was glamorous.

She is completely honest. She says what she thinks and does what she likes. She does not conform to the conventional mind. A man can get away with it—but a woman can't. So says Joan, about her dynamic sister

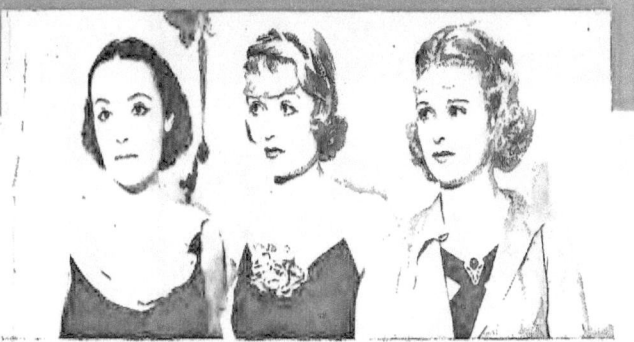

At the left, Joan Bennett, a star in her own right, who writes this story of her sister. And on this page, Joan and Constance, snapped with Dolores Del Rio at the Mayfair Ball at the Beverly-Wilshire Hotel.

Drawings by
Henri Weiner

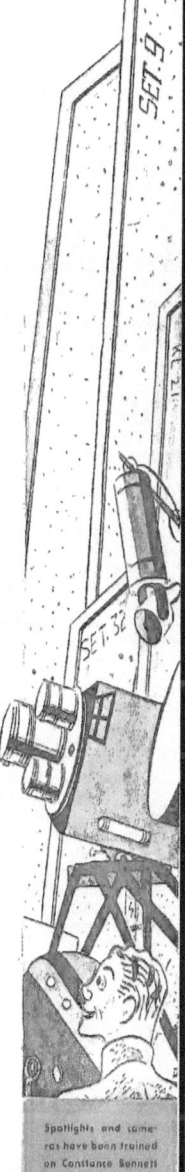

Spotlights and cameras have been trained on Constance Bennett since she was a child. They are in her blood.

She was the leader in every crowd. Everything she did was done with dash and fire and imagination. She never entered a room, she swept in—and instantly took command of the situation. She never passed through the "gangly" stage, for her poise was too instinctive to permit self-consciousness. She was very popular.

As a child she was extremely precocious. She soaked up knowledge as effortlessly as a sponge soaks up water. Unlike most so-called precocious children, she was analytical. Instead of being content to skim the surface, she wanted to know the reason why. She still does. Moreover, her mind is amazingly retentive. Once having fixed on an idea, she never forgets.

The fact that she was a girl was a bitter disappointment to our father, who had set his heart on a son who would carry on in his footsteps. Being one of the most wilful men that ever lived, he refused to become reconciled to the fact of her sex for years. Consequently, he treated Constance as he would have treated a son.

She already had, by inheritance, his fighting heart, his impatience with all restraint, his wilfullness—and he encouraged her in every one of those qualities. He took her into his confidence, treated her as though she were an adult, instilled into her mind his own arrogant, "self-made man's" psychology. He preached the necessity of learning by experience, of fighting one's own battles, of being able to "take it on the chin" without a whine.

One of the immediate results was, of course, that her will began to clash with his while she was still a child. It has continued to clash with his ever since, in a series of explosions which are usually short-lived but breath-taking in their violence. Father frequently rages when she defies his authority—yet I know he is tremendously proud of her determination and independence.

He has ample reason to be proud of her courage. I have never seen her afraid of anything—unless it might be that she is sometimes afraid of being afraid.

I have never seen her shirk a fight, no matter how slim her chance of winning might be. She welcomes and heartily enjoys the stimulation of conflict. A torrid argument is to her one of life's supreme joys, an escape from boredom, which she cannot tolerate. She is quick to show her withering contempt for anyone who fails to stick to his guns. She is also quick to acknowledge her fault, once she has been convinced that she is wrong.

If there is any one thing which Constance detests more than all others, that thing is a "yes-man." Anyone who wishes to hold her respect and liking must have the courage of his convictions and be willing to pit them against hers. She admires a fighter. And give her credit for this: if her temper is quickly kindled, it also is quickly quenched.

She neither expects nor wants anyone to grovel before her opinions because she happens to be a star; neither will she be subservient to anyone because of that person's position. Many stars "red-apple" the producers; Connie's Hollywood career has been punctuated by her challenges to their judgment and authority. I honestly believe that she would turn her back on stardom, salary and everything else which Hollywood can offer her before she would "yes" a producer against her convictions.

Her first starring contract was only a few days old when she asserted her independence. Her producers had gone into a huddle with their publicity executives and determined on a campaign in her behalf. When her boat docked in New York (she had signed her contract in Paris), she found awaiting her a telegram which virtually ordered her to cooperate by giving out a story entitled "No Girl Should Marry a Millionaire." Instantly she wired back:

". . . . I refuse to crash the front pages in that way. For some inexplicable reason, when I come to America, I always land on the front pages—and without having to make an ass of myself to do it!"

Constance did not exaggerate. She has been front page copy ever since she was a girl in school.

No one has been more misrepresented by the press than she has been. Whenever she has been maligned, she has instantly fought back. Last year she filed no less than four libel suits against magazines and newspapers. Probably her prompt resentment has aroused the enmity of a few publishers, but, in her lexicon, better an enemy than the sacrifice of one's self-respect!

Reporters have stormed because she refuses to grant interviews while she is working in a picture, and because she will not see any writer without first knowing his intended subject. She feels that she is justified in both stands. Never strong physically, she devotes so much energy to her work that, during production, she has no reserve left to bestow on interviewers.

If I have portrayed Constance as a fire-brand who constantly carries a chip on her shoulder, I have failed in my purpose. She is a fire-brand, but she carries no chip. She never avoids a fight, but neither does she provoke one.

Unlike most combative persons, she has a flair for logic which acts as a balance wheel. She arrives at her conclusions with amazing celerity, but never without due thought and the careful weighing of one factor against another.

It is that sense of logic, plus her decisiveness, which makes her a magnificent business woman. She has always been the generalissimo of her own affairs. She seeks advice, but reserves and exercises the right to value it against her own opinions and reach her own decisions. She employs a business counsellor, but make no mistake about this: it is Constance who utters the final word, whether the question in hand involves a new studio contract or a stock market investment.

In the administration of her home, she pays close attention to every detail. She examines every bill, decides upon every expenditure, determines every menu. How she finds the time and energy to do so, even during the stress of picture-making, has always been a mystery to me. Why, I have known her to spend hours phrasing and re-phrasing an answer to one of her fan letters. It must express exactly her intended meaning before it is allowed to enter the mail.

It has been said, with considerable justice, that most screen stars are the product of at least a dozen brains; Constance is the product of just one—her own!

She has a keen, though very caustic, sense of humor. At times, she is cuttingly sarcastic—and since she is a genius for seeing through affectation, her sarcasms are usually as penetrating as a surgeon's lance.

Connie Should Have Been a Boy

Even as a child, Connie could not stomach affectation. People who "put on a front" have always disgusted her—and she finds a perverse delight in stripping off their masks. Pretence and insincerity being a vogue in Hollywood, it is easy to understand why many poseurs in the picture colony fear and dislike her.

One of her worst faults is intolerance. Most issues, to her, are clear-cut, and she lacks the patience to seek excuses for other people's actions and beliefs. Above all else, she is intolerant of stupidity. An unintelligent person bores her insufferably—and, again, she lacks the patience to disguise her boredom. She resents bitterly and volubly, anything which she considers an "insult to my intelligence" (the phrase is hers). In that resentment lies the cause of many of her quarrels with the press. I remember a story published several years ago, which asserted that she spends $250,000 annually on her clothes. It threw her into a rage.

"I don't care what they write about me so long as they don't insult my intelligence like this!" she stormed.

Characteristically, her anger burned until she had answered. Constance can never be content until she has had an eye for an eye. Step on her toes, and she will treasure the injury jealously until it is repaid, with interest.

To continue with her faults; she is, I think, too egotistic, too determined to have her own way, no matter what or who must be over-ridden in obtaining it. Life has been prodigal in its treatment of her. True, she has unusual intelligence, unusual ability, unusual capacity for work, unusual force of character—but she has also been extraordinarily lucky. She has no conception of the meaning of poverty. She has never been forced to impose upon her own inclinations the restraints mothered by Necessity. As a consequence, she is apt to be—and sometimes is—to be inconsiderate of others who have been less fortunate.

Again, her psychology is that of a man . . . and, in a man it would be more generally understood. She takes what she wants!

Yet, paradoxically, she wants to be kind and helpful to every creature less fortunate than herself. I know of many things which she has done for unfortunates—and I know better than to recount them here, for I would only invite a quarrel with Connie. She has been criticized, and she is proud—consequently, she disdains to cite in her own behalf any of the countless good deeds which might confound her critics.

Her sympathies are quickly and deeply touched—if she considers the object worthy of sympathy. If not, she can be quite merciless.

She has always been too quick to judge people. Even as a child, she either liked, or disliked—and there were no half-tones in her appraisals. Maturity has strengthened, rather than weakened, that trait. But it is amazing how correct her judgments usually are.

To those whom she loves, Constance is loyal, almost to a fault. Despite her independence, she is intensely loyal to her family—to "the Bennetts." During his recent illness, she sacrificed all her own interests to be with Father, night and day. Time and again, she has rushed half-way around the earth to "stand-by" when some member of the family needed her.

She is proud, I believe, of the theatrical traditions of the family—although I have never heard her express that feeling in so many words. As a matter of fact, she prefers to talk about acting, stardom and everything else pertaining to her profession from the standpoint of hard-boiled business. But I remember the eagerness she invariably displayed when she and Barbara and I, as kids, played theater. When she married Philip Plant, it was with the avowed intention of never acting again, but, even so, I think she was unable to shake the conviction that her real career remained before the cameras.

THAT she has been able to achieve so much has always been a source of amazement to me, for, physically, she has never been strong. In her case, ambition and nervous energy have combined to drive her body far beyond its natural powers. Physicians have often warned her to "take it easy," but they have advised the impossible. Constance is a dynamo. Idleness, in her estimation, is stagnation, and stagnation she cannot stand. She must be forever on the move, driving forward, picking up new experiences, new stimuli. And, characteristically, she drives others.

She lives now—and always has lived—with regal magnificence. She denies herself nothing that she wants, yet, surprisingly, her wants are comparatively simple. In many things, she is extravagant, in others she is very saving.

Brilliant, yet logical; intolerant, yet sympathetic; combative, yet quick to admit an error; poised, yet unaffected—Constance has as many facets as a well-cut diamond.

But I like best to think of her as I—and few others—have seen her in the privacy of her home with Peter Plant, her son. I like to see the eagerness with which he runs to her on her entrance and the unfailing patience with which she shares all of his troubles and his joys.

And like all the Bennetts, I'm very proud of Constance, who is neither perfect—nor wants to be considered so!

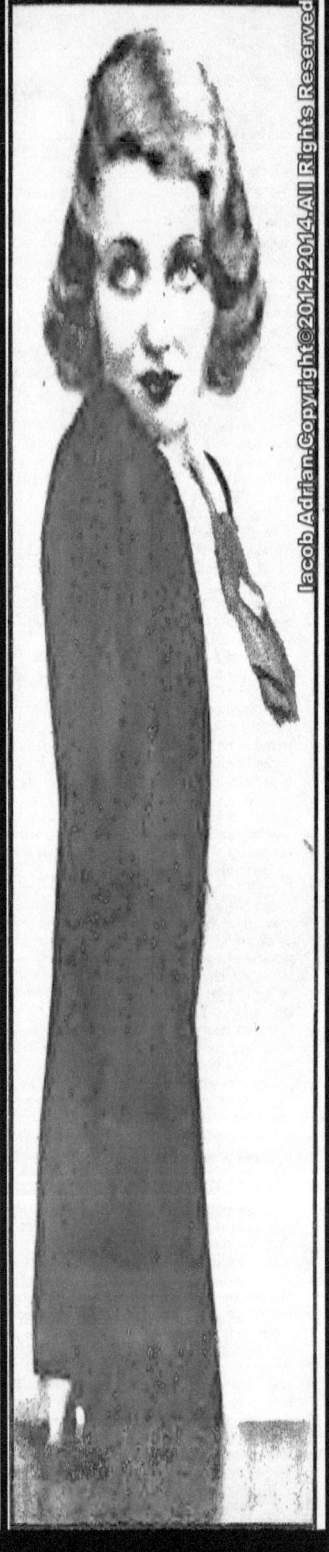

Jacob Adrian Copyright © 2012-2014 All Rights Reserved

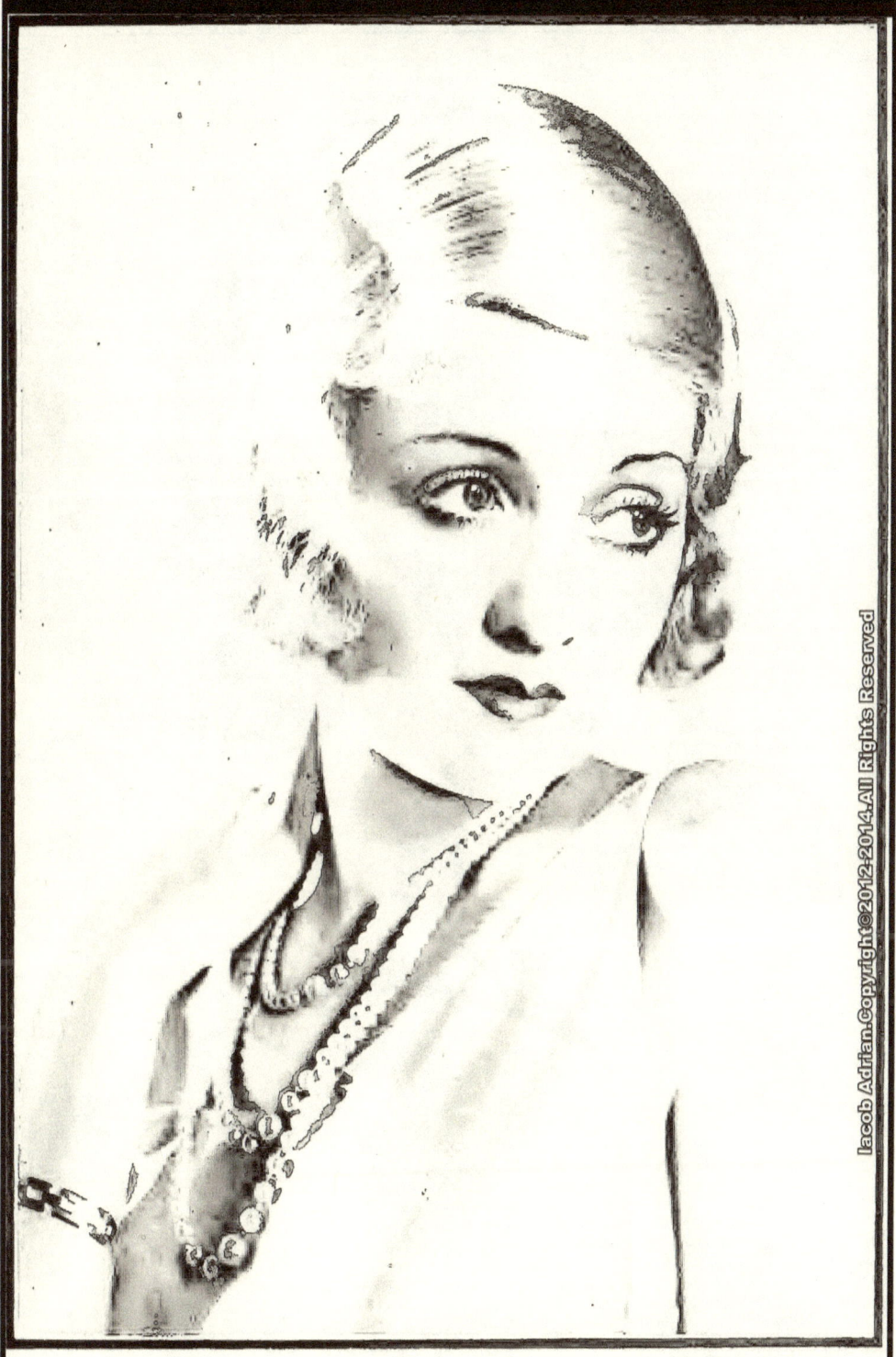

CONSTANCE BENNETT

Iacob Adrian Copyright©2012-2014 All Rights Reserved

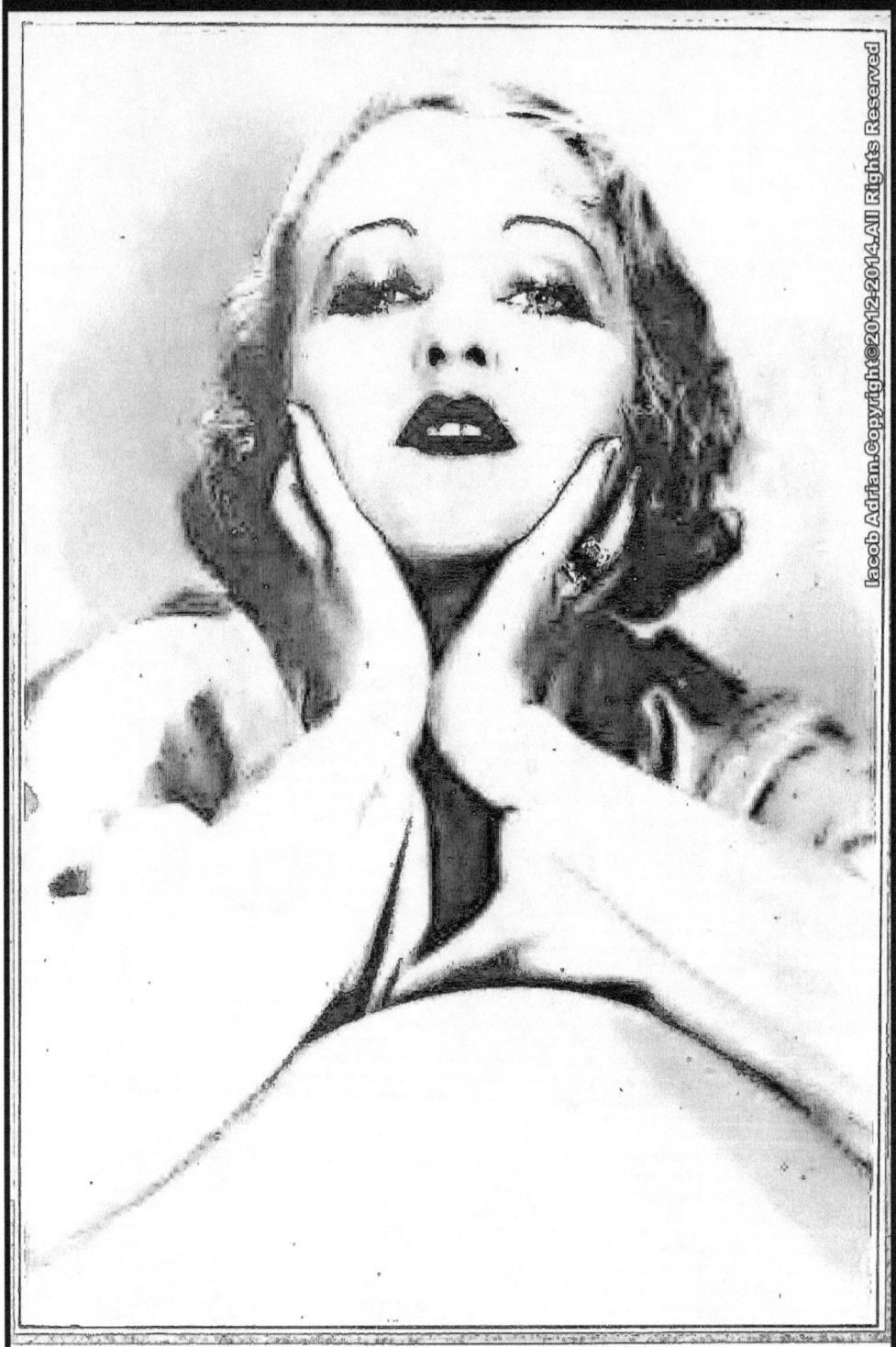

Iacob Adrian Copyright©2012-2014 All Rights Reserved

CONSTANCE BENNETT

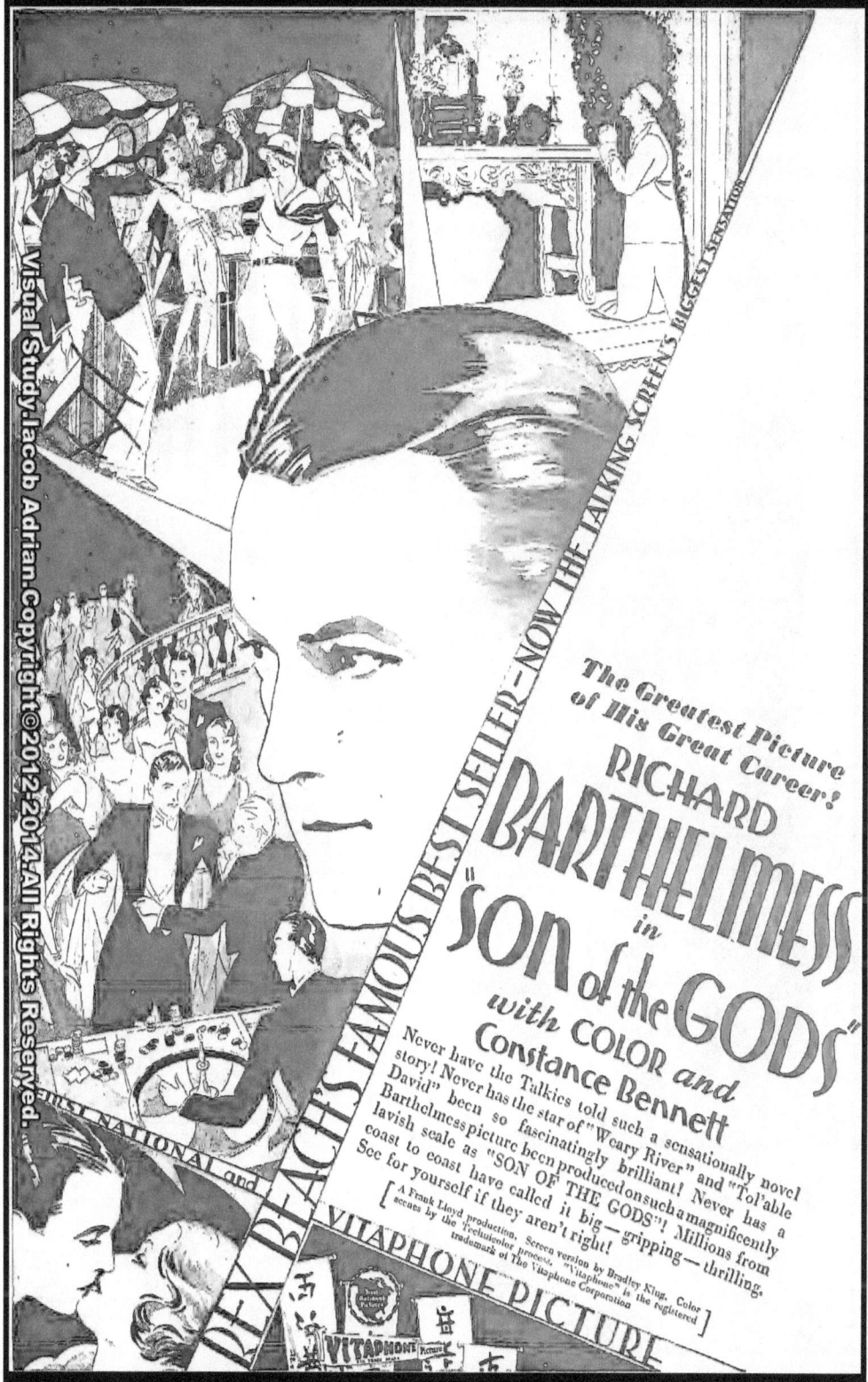

Visual Study Jacob Adrian Copyright©2012-2014.All Rights Reserved.

The Greatest Picture
of His Great Career!

RICHARD
BARTHELMESS
in
"SON of the GODS"
with COLOR and
Constance Bennett

REX BEACH'S FAMOUS BEST SELLER—NOW THE TALKING SCREEN'S BIGGEST SENSATION

Never have the Talkies told such a sensational novel
story! Never has the star of "Weary River" and "Tol'able
David" been so fascinatingly brilliant! Never has a
Barthelmess picture been produced on such a magnificently
lavish scale as "SON OF THE GODS"! Millions from
coast to coast have called it big — gripping — thrilling'
See for yourself if they aren't right!

[A Frank Lloyd production. Screen version by Bradley King, Color
scenes by the Technicolor process. "Vitaphone" is the registered
trademark of the Vitaphone Corporation]

FIRST NATIONAL and VITAPHONE PICTURE

VITAPHONE
Picture

The HIGH HAT GIRL

BY ADELA ROGERS ST. JOHNS

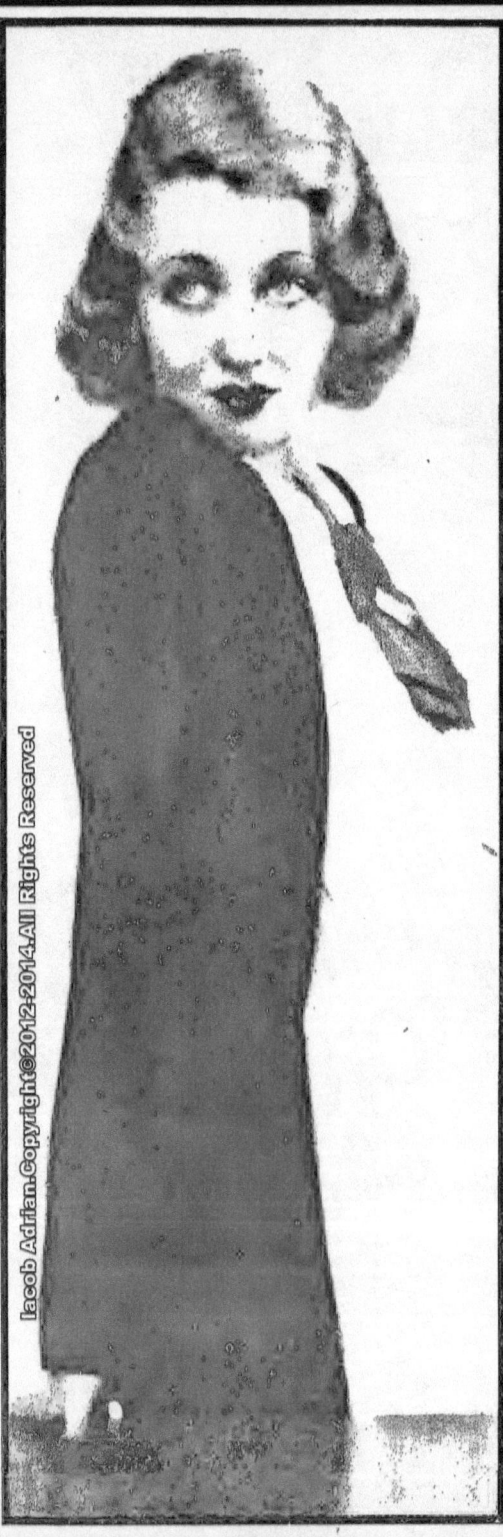

Iacob Adrian Copyright©2012-2014 All Rights Reserved

IT is a long time since anyone dared to wear a high hat in Hollywood.

The wits and the wisecrackers have practically eliminated that particular piece of headgear. They laugh. And they begin pertinent remarks with "Why, I remember when—" A high hat is the favorite target for verbal bullets laden with ridicule and sarcasm.

A few stage importations have attempted it and taken it off in a hurry.

Constance Bennett wears one and gets away with it. In fact, Hollywood rather seems to like it. The blond and haughty Constance has intrigued Hollywood as nobody has done for years.

There are two reasons for that. First, she does it so darn well, and the picture colony generously concedes admiration to anyone who makes a bluff stick. Second, she has provided a new topic of conversation. Any dinner party can be saved by hurling forth this one remark: "How does Constance Bennett get that way?"

I DON'T like unanswered questions floating about. One has been trained by modern literature to believe all mysteries solvable. So I started a small private investigation regarding Constance Bennett, the high hat girl of Hollywood.

And uncovered some amazing things.

"How does Constance Bennett get that way?"

There is about her an air of arrogance, almost an air of tragedy. For months I have watched the beauty from a safe distance. Never did I see her smile. Sitting amid the friendly, noisy throng at lunch in the Brown Derby, her eyes are the eyes of a disdainful goddess forced to watch mere mortals at play.

Constance Bennett asks nothing of anybody, she feels free to live according to her own lights. Much of her manner is defensive, protective. This girl has the honest lack of enthusiasm of her generation.

Riding through the streets of Beverly Hills in her car, she suggests a duchess of Marie Antoinette's reign on her way to be presented to that plebeian upstart, Napoleon.

At a dinner party

It's a Long Time Since Anyone in Hollywood Dared to Wear One—but Constance Bennett Is a Modern Young Woman Who Cares Nothing About the Opinion of the Multitude

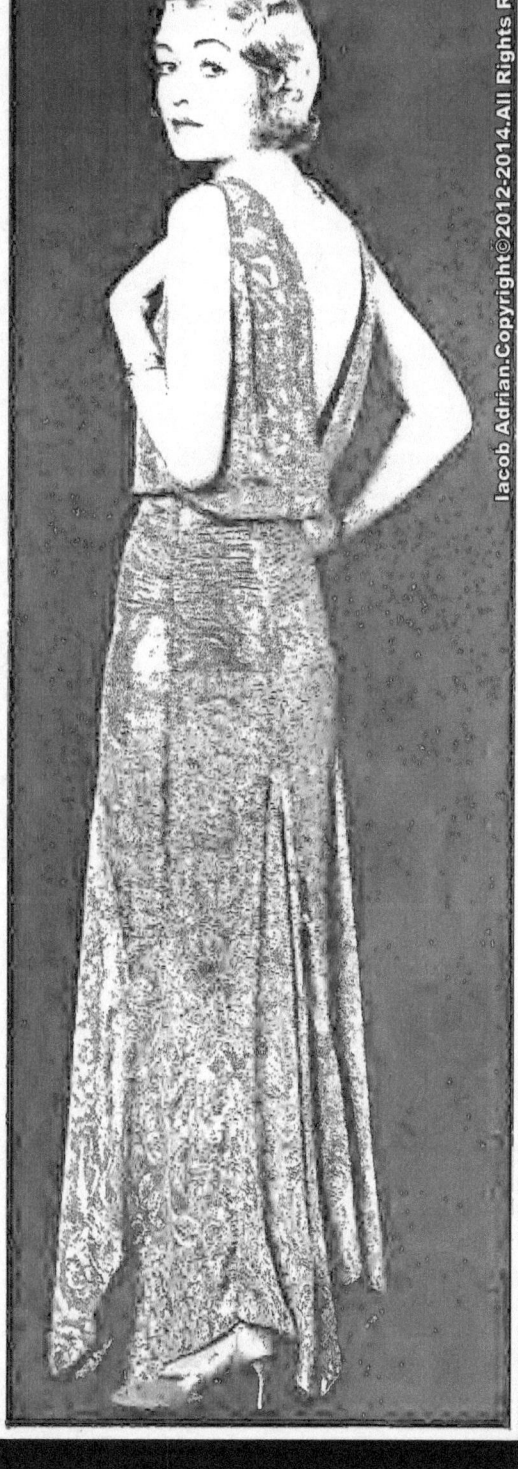

the other evening, I sat directly across from her. It was a very gay dinner party. The Ambassador's famous Cocoanut Grove was bright with many colored lights. Melody filled the air. Around the table, massed with gorgeous flowers, wit and laughter flowed.

Dolores Del Rio sparkled with jewels and with merriment. Bebe Daniels, with Ben Lyon beside her, was radiant with that sheer joy of living which makes her irresistible. Constance Talmadge, whom one sees so seldom since her happy marriage to Townsend Netcher, was keeping everyone within earshot stimulated and gay.

Constance Bennett was different. She seemed wrapt in veils of delicate mystery. Aloof, gorgeous, a little bored perhaps. Even when she danced, no single ripple touched the hauteur of her face. Over the black shoulder of her partner she stared into space, the same weary disdain touching her lovely mouth.

Beside me was a young man who for reasons of gallantry must be nameless. Suffice it to say that on two continents he is famous for his wit. And his understanding of human nature.

"What," I said to him at last, "is the burden that rests upon Miss Bennett's beautiful back? I am at heart a Pollyanna. I like to see everyone happy. Isn't it considered the thing these days to be gay and gallant, no matter how disillusioned one may be?"

"I think," he said, "that the tragic expression comes from the strain of trying to balance a high hat. Jugglers are ever of solemn countenance. And compared to wearing a high hat in this town keeping nineteen saucers in the air is mere child's play."

But I had determined to see Miss Bennett, in my professional capacity, and try to find out about all this.

BY the time the head studio press agent had told the personal press agent, who told the secretary, who consulted the business manager, who advised the personal maid, who informed somebody else that I wished an appointment with Miss Constance Bennett herself, the whole thing began to pall upon me a trifle.

The truth is that one has been spoiled, said I to myself.

One has been spoiled by the exquisite graciousness and the all-embracing kindliness of a Marion Davies, who entertains Lindbergh, the Baron de Rothschild, Lady Mountbatten and Mayor James J. Walker. By the simplicity and gentle dignity of a Mary Pickford, who

Constance Bennett's success was made in arrogant, vivid, high hat sort of parts, suited perfectly to her appearance and manner. The public loved them. Miss Bennett is a type we understand today, sensational, intriguing, fascinating.

Jacob Adrian.Copyright©2012-2014.All Rights Reserved

The Girl Who Cares Nothing for Personal Popularity

is the honored guest of kings. By the warmth and shyness of a Colleen Moore, the hail-fellow-well-met g o o d nature of a Clara Bow, even by the slightly awkward and reserved courtesy of Garbo.

Why, said I again to myself, should Constance Bennett be high hat?

I thought of a number of reasons and eliminated them.

It couldn't be just because she was so startlingly attractive to look at. After all, Corinne Griffith s t i l l moves her charming and natural way among us. Billie Dove is still unassuming a n d rather wistfully envious of girls with no beauty who are given credit for brains.

It couldn't be because she had achieved a tremendous success so suddenly in pictures. That happened to little Janet Gaynor without affecting her girlish sweetness and simplicity in the least.

Surely not the fact that she wears her

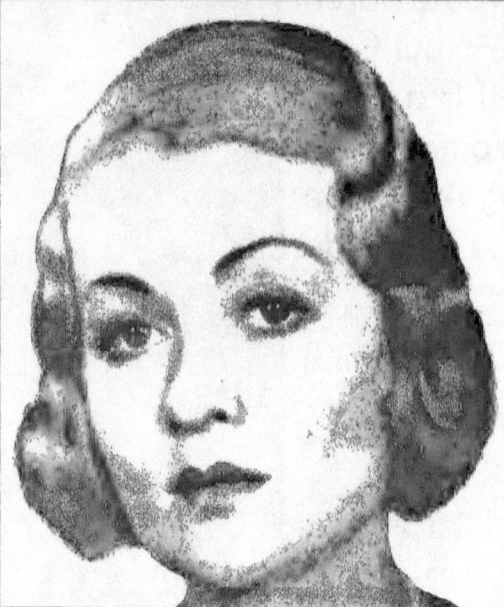

Constance is Richard Bennett's own daughter. .The American stage has seen few better actors than Richard Bennett. No one knew that better than Richard Bennett himself—self-confidence was almost a religion with him. Constance is amazingly like her father.

manners, and she has many moods. Her behavior, after the modern fashion, comes entirely from within.

And it happens that she doesn't care for people nor for the opinion of the multitude—also a distinctly modern trait. Since she asks nothing of anybody, she feels free to live according to her own lights. The world as a whole she disdains somewhat, not from any sense of superiority, but from that too-mature knowledge of the world which gives so many young women of our day the feeling that life is rather a mess anyhow.

MUCH of her grand manner is defensive, protective. The problem which nearly every woman with a career faces—the problem of waste, in time, money, energy—is most easily met for her by wearing an armor of indifference. The indifference isn't feigned. She isn't particularly

marvelous clothes with a dash and style that is perfect. There is Gloria Swanson, who is still without equal when it comes to clothes. And Lilyan Tashman. And Ruth Chatterton. And the elegantly gowned and meticulously groomed Norma Shearer.

OF course, she can act. "Son of the Gods" will not soon be forgotten. But then, there is Garbo, there is Gaynor, there is Bebe Daniels. No performance in a long time equaled Swanson's in "The Trespasser."

It may be true, she has a million dollars in the bank. But millions are not unknown among our picture stars. Colleen Moore has *earned* much more than that. Mary Pickford and Betty Compson are both millionaires. So are the Talmadges. Money hasn't overpowered any of them.

Can't be social standing, because of the Plants. Bebe Daniels owns a family tree which would admit her to any social register. Dolores Del Rio held a high position both in Mexico and Europe. June Collyer was a New York débutante and Junior Leaguer.

Not a high hat in the bunch.

I was baffled.

And while I still pondered, the groceryman — we haven't yet a postman at Malibu Beach—brought me a large, gray envelope addressed in a fashionable distinguished hand.

It has been my privilege to receive a number of charming notes. But I never received one more charming than this one signed Constance Bennett. Simple, gracious, courteous. An apology for a seeming rudeness. Would I come for luncheon any day? She had dismissed the servants whose carelessness had resulted in a misunderstanding so unnecessary.

Frankly, I was amazed. But it led to enlightenment in many directions upon Connie Bennett.

She is a modern of moderns. Her moods are her

excited about anything, sees nothing in life to be excited about. There is a hard, philosophical calm about her generation, an honest lack of enthusiasm. This girl possesses it to the nth degree.

Also, she is Richard Bennett's own daughter. The American stage has seen few better actors than Richard Bennett. No one knew that better than Richard Bennett himself. Self-confidence was almost a religion with him. In looks, temperament and ability, Constance is amazingly like her father. She has always been his favorite.

I remember when Constance was a youngster and Dick Bennett was starring in stock in Los Angeles. She was his constant companion. He preached to her the gospel of survival—that the world will lick you unless you lick it first. He told her that success can be satisfactory only if built entirely upon ability. Be so good they *have* to recognize you. Then demand your share of the rewards.

I think there is in Constance Bennett much of the idea that life will hurt you badly if you get too friendly with it.

Being a modern, she knows instinctively and consciously the value of type. There is a principle which everyone in pictures must grasp or fail. There is no error like stepping out of character.

THE IT girl, Clara Bow, can do many things which would ruin Janet Gaynor over night. That's what people expect of the great exponent of sex appeal. Scandals which would only augmented the fascination of Barbara La Marr would be completely fatal to Mary Brian.

Constance Bennett came from Paris to Hollywood to go back into pictures. No one paid much attention. Her success was rapid and rather astounding. The parts she played were far from sympathetic — acting parts, full of character and

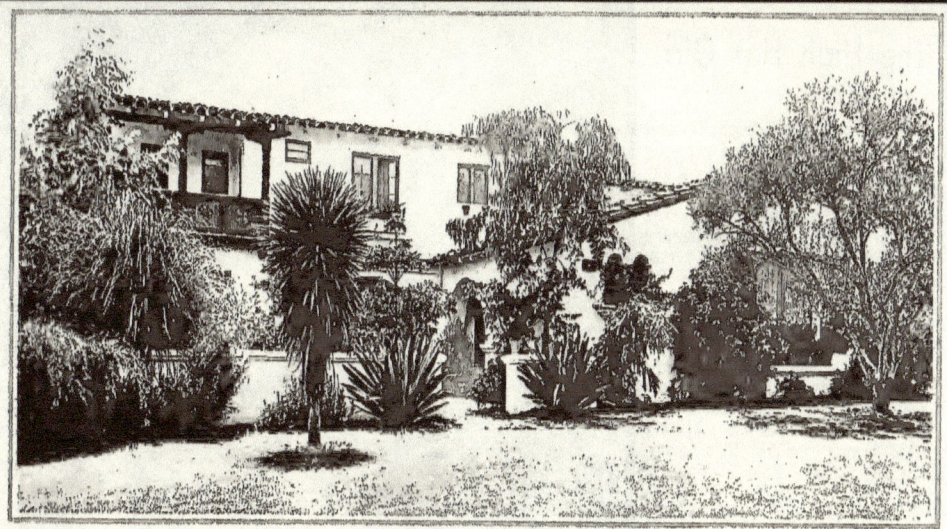

Constance Bennett's home in Beverly Hills

HOW HOLLYWOOD ENTERTAINS

BY
EVELYN GRAY

Photographs by Stagg

ONCE in a while everyone gets tired of big parties. And girls who really like to play bridge and play a good game like nothing better than an intimate foursome. A light, early lunch and a long quiet afternoon for their rubbers appeals to many of the bridge-players in Hollywood.

Constance Bennett, who as Mrs. Phillip Plant was well known as a hostess both in New York and Paris, gives one of these small bridge luncheons about once a week. She prefers it to any other method of daytime entertaining and does it perfectly. Her charming new home in Beverly Hills is admirably suited to any at home hospitality.

THE other afternoon she had a bridge luncheon just for four. Luncheon was served promptly at twelve

o'clock. The dining room table, however, was formally prepared and gave the occasion quite a "party" atmosphere. There were vases of brilliant zinnias, exquisite little French embroidered doilies at each place and Wedgwood serving (*Continued on page* 113)

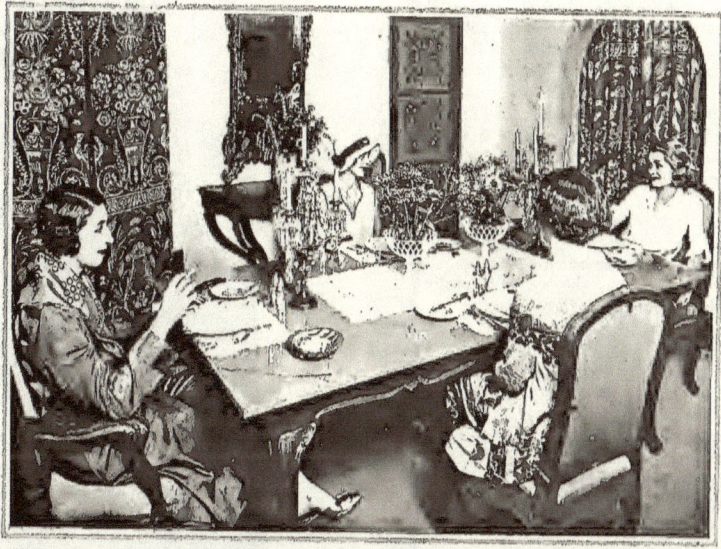

Miss Bennett's bridge foursome: left, to right Mrs. Barney Glazer, Mrs. Jules Glaenzer, Mrs. Adela Rogers Hyland (back to camera), and Miss Bennett.

The High Hat Girl

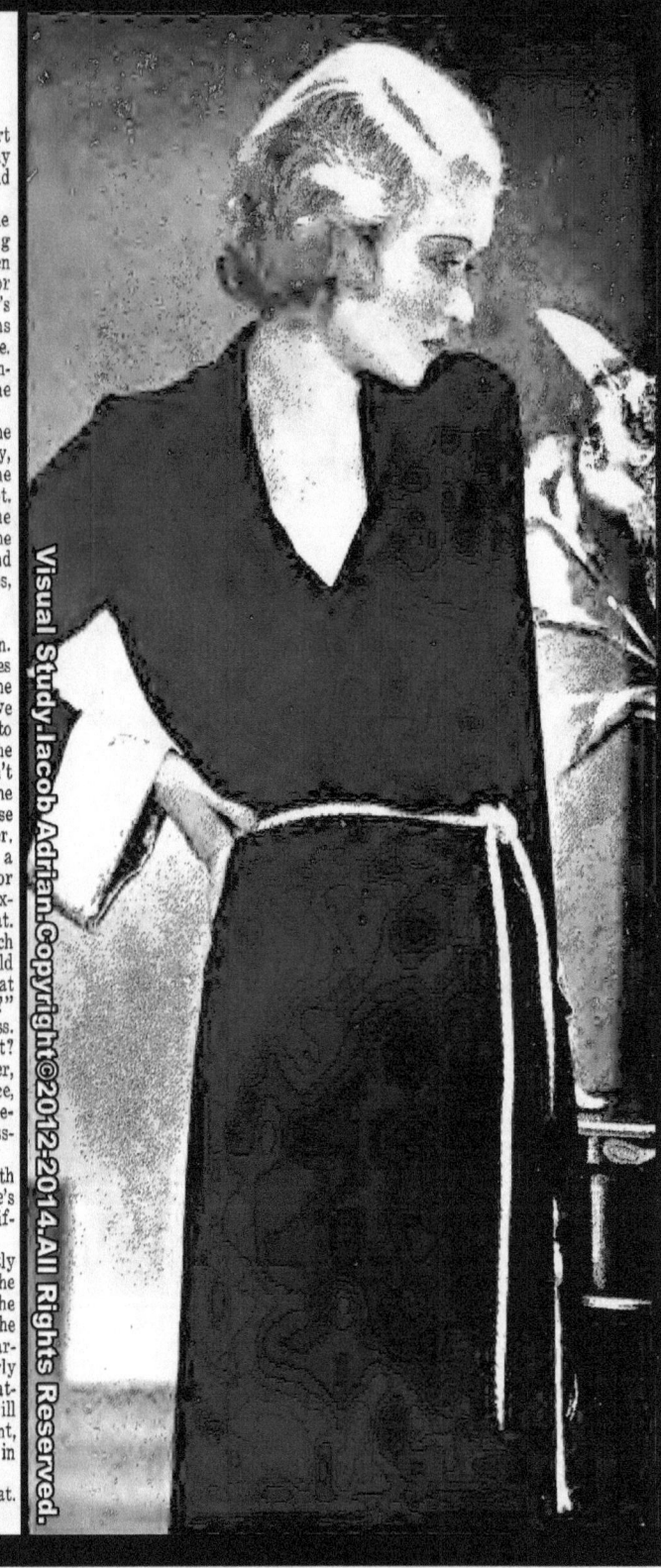

color. Arrogant, vivid, high hat sort of parts they were. Suited perfectly to Constance Bennett's appearance and manner.

Well, they were successful. The public loved them. Why be something different off the screen? Great screen figures rise and gain popularity for many reasons. Constance Bennett's fan mail is enormous, her name means coin of the realm at the box-office. Why? Because she is a type we completely understand today, because she is sensational, intriguing, fascinating.

In many ways, she is more like the modern young woman than many, many other stars. I don't think she cares whether she is popular or not. With the complete cynicism of the modern, she shrugs at the favor of the majority. "Today you're a hero and tomorrow you're a bum," she quotes, smiling.

SHE amuses herself when she can. She works because frankly she loves acting, and she loves fame, and the things money buys. Her illusions have long since vanished and she refuses to pretend to any. Freedom to do as she pleases is important to her. She hasn't the natural instinct to please, and she refuses to waste time trying to please people who don't mean anything to her.

I am sure Constance Bennett isn't a very happy person. The capacity for happiness isn't hers to any great extent. Some people are made like that. Constance Bennett doesn't spend much time chasing the bluebird. If you told her that she would probably say, "What would I do with a bluebird if I got it?" But she accepts life without bitterness. There it is. What can you do about it?

Her charm lies, when you know her, largely in this complete indifference, this effective honesty. There is something soothing in its lack of restlessness.

Whatever you do is all right with her. You've got your life to live. She's got hers. If you choose to do it in different ways, why bother each other?

The high hat she wears is partly armor from the annoyances of the world, partly the natural manner of the Bennetts, partly indifference. She doesn't worry about personal popularity because she doesn't particularly want it. She knows, what all very attractive women know, that she will never lack companionship, amusement, entertainment, while there are men in the world.

And that, as the English say, is that.

Visual Study.Jacob Adrian.Copyright©2012-2014.All Rights Reserved.

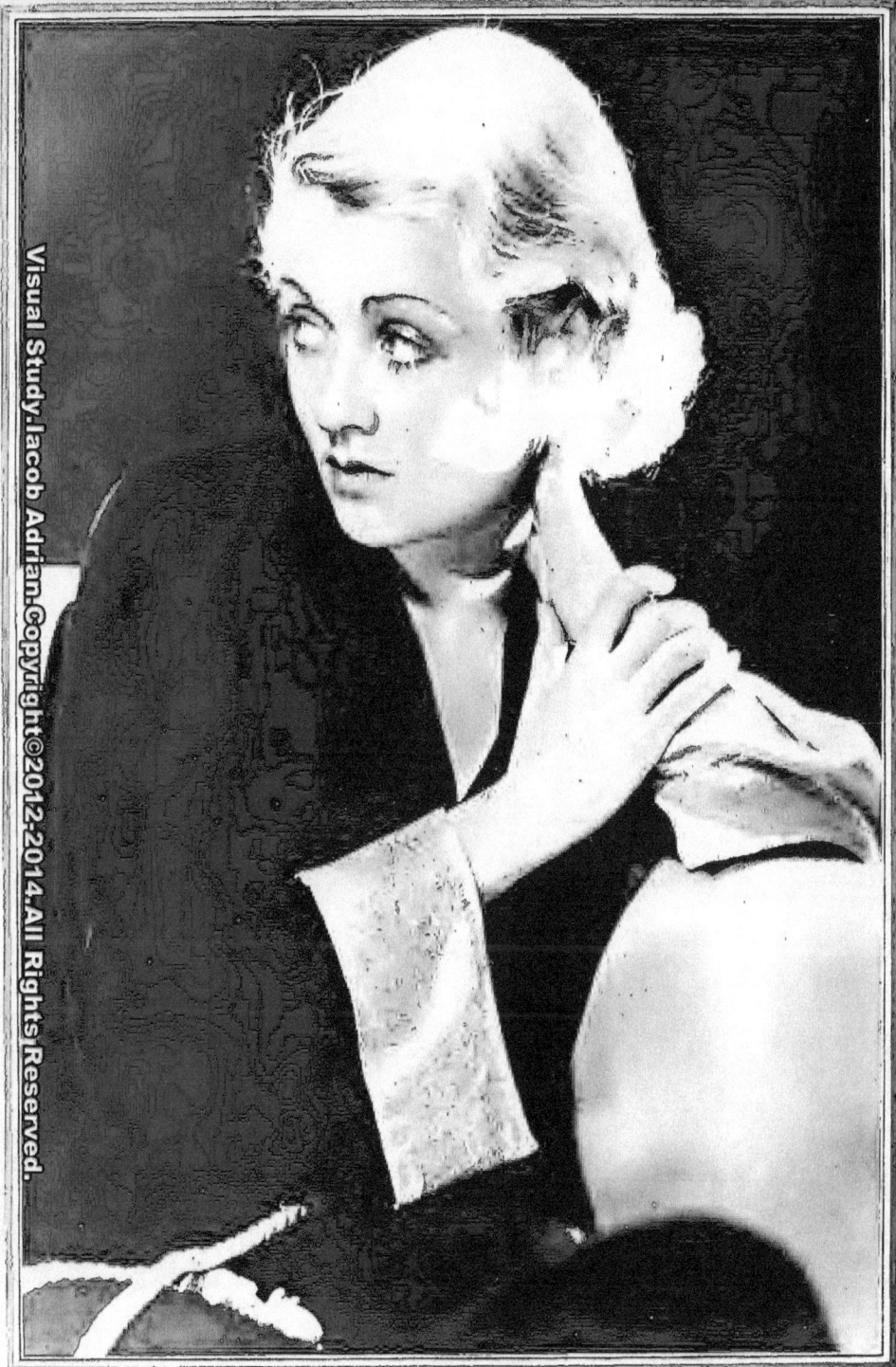

Visual Study.Jacob Adrian.Copyright©2012-2014.All Rights Reserved.

CONSTANCE BENNETT

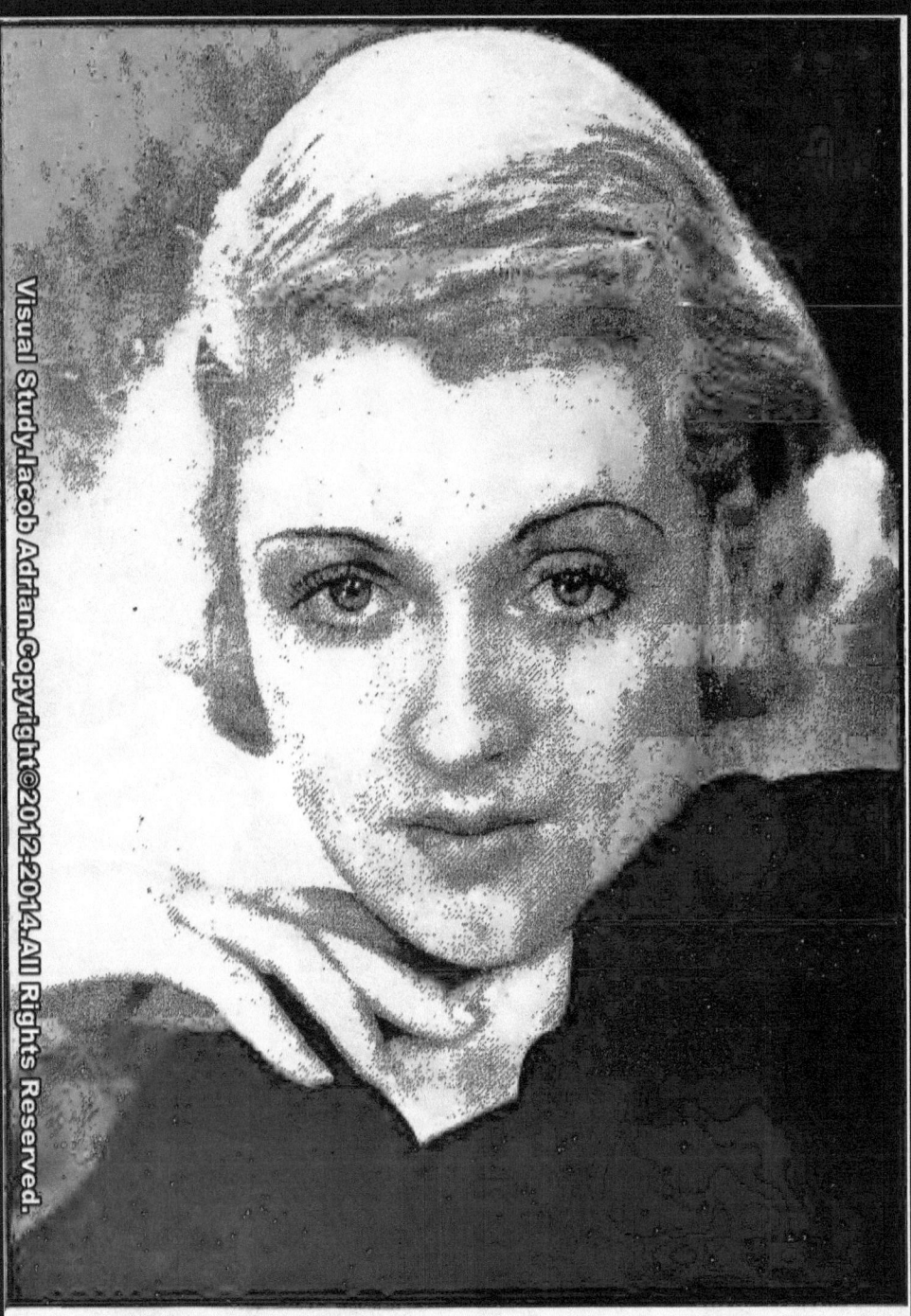

Visual Study.Jacob Adrian.Copyright©2012-2014.All Rights Reserved.

Constance Bennett returned to the screen late in 1929 after a four years' absence. Her new success has been remarkable. Miss Bennett has been painted by Hollywood interviewers as hard, high hat, and heartless. In reality, says Mr. Mook, she is none of the things she has been called. And, across the page, he tells you of the childhood that developed the Constance Bennett of 1931, one of the most popular of all talkie stars.

The Romance of the
COMET GIRL

The Story of Movieland's Newest Meteor, Constance Bennett, Who Has Flashed Into Prominence in New York, Paris and Hollywood

By S. R. MOOK

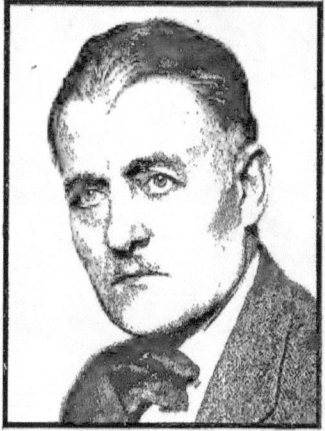

Richard Bennett, father of Constance, Joan and Barbara Bennett. He has been a stage actor and star for years.

Wide World

NEW MOVIE is to present—in three parts—the dramatic story of Constance Bennett. The chapter this month deals with her childhood and her first marriage. Next month NEW MOVIE will tell of Miss Bennett's early screen adventures and her marriage to Phil Plant, the young millionaire.

Miss Bennett's story is a fascinating one. Daughter of a famous stage family, her childhood was both colorful and varied. The unexpected always lurked around the corner.

A YEAR and a half ago Constance Bennett returned to the screen after a four years' absence. Immediately interviews broke all over the country—magazines, newspapers, periodicals of all sorts.

"Every Girl Should Marry a Millionaire!"
"$250,000 a Year on Clothes!"
"What Love Means to Me!"
"The High Hat Girl of Hollywood."

There was scarcely a magazine in the country chronicling motion picture personalities which did not carry a story about her. And the amazing part was that few of them were complimentary and, according to Constance, even fewer of them accurate.

I had known her intermittently since she was possibly five years old. The girl I had known seemed to fit none of the articles describing

a girl who was supposed to be brilliant and heartless. The girl I had known was warm and sympathetic. It didn't seem possible she could have changed so much.

I RECALLED an incident that occurred when she was possibly nine years old. Her family was living out on Long Island. Her father had given her a bird dog for a present. It was the first time she had ever owned a dog all her own. The family had always had pets, but they had been more or less community property to be shared with her sisters. This was exclusively hers. She lavished affection on the animal and the dog adored her. They were playing on the sidewalk in front of her home one afternoon when the dog darted into the street after a ball she had thrown. An automobile ran over him. Connie gave him one stricken look and flew down the street to a veterinary's. She returned with the slightly bewildered gentleman in tow. The dog, seeing her coming, wriggled over to her and died with his head in her lap.

Connie was inconsolable. Her grief found an outlet in

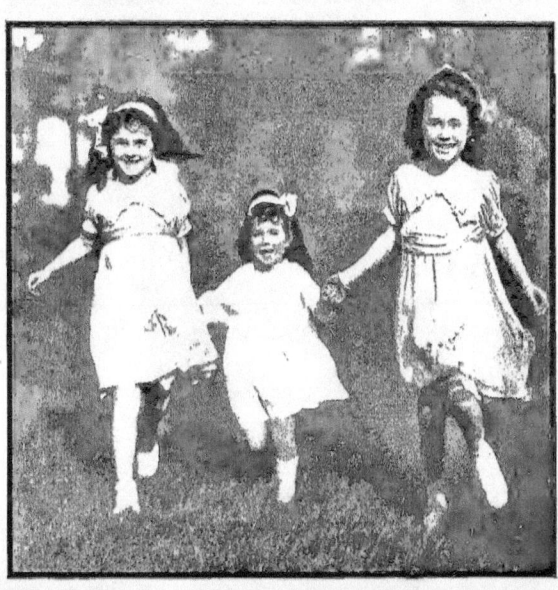

A childhood picture of the Bennett girls. Left to right, Barbara, Joan and Constance.

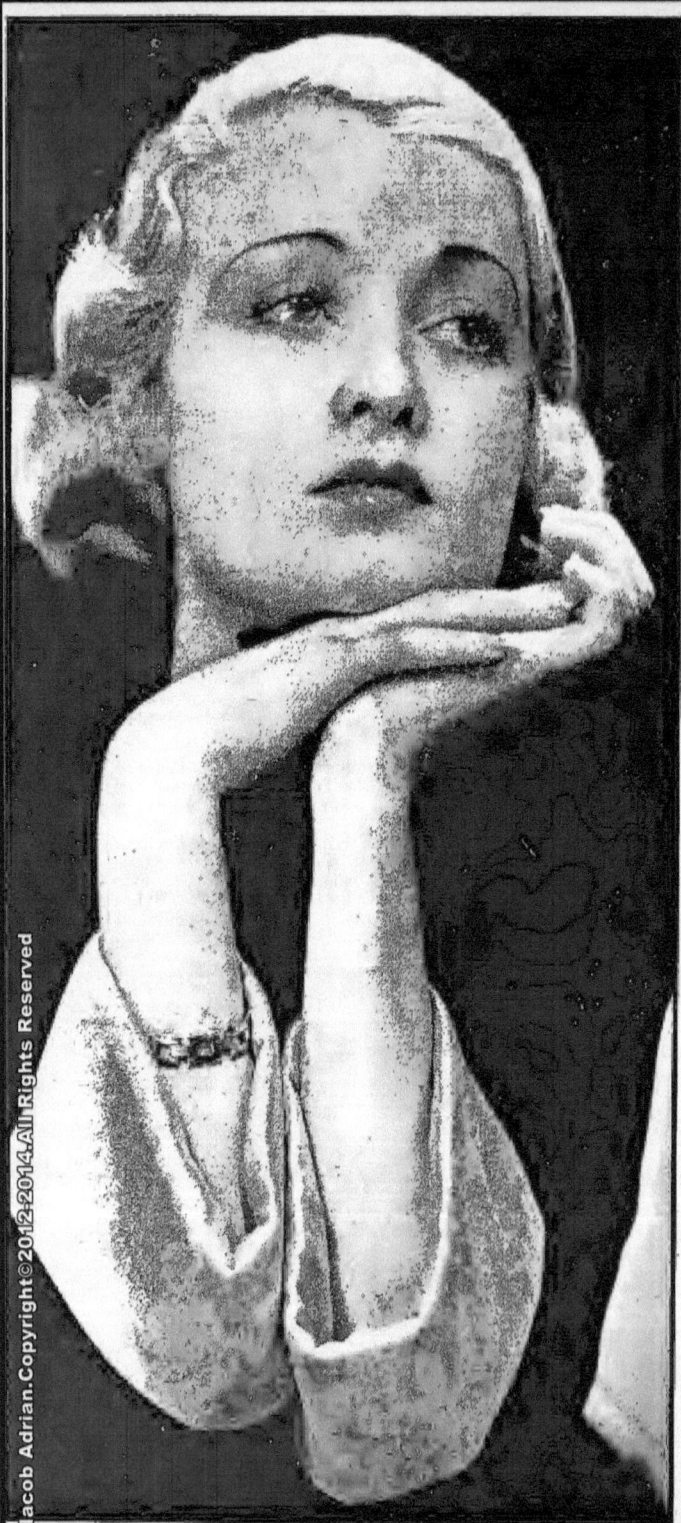

Jacob Adrian.Copyright©2012-2014.All Rights Reserved

poetry. It was her first offence in that direction and the result was called "Ode to a Lost Dog." She still writes poetry and has had a number of verses published anonymously.

Her love of dogs has persisted ever since. The den in her home today contains a collection of miniature porcelain dogs that must be the despair of the maid who has to dust them. And Connie cannot pass one in a store without buying it.

AS a child there was something grave and dignified about her. She insists that her childhood was just like any other child's — but it wasn't.

Her father was—and is— an unusually successful stage actor, but he has always been erratic and eccentric. When I was thirteen or fourteen and as stage struck as they come, I was horrified to read in a theatrical trade paper that Mr. Bennett had refused to be starred by the Lieblers, who were among the biggest producers of those days. I immediately wrote him a letter of expostulation, pointing out that he could make much more money if he were starred and that he owed it to his wife and three charming children to make as much as he could.

He must have recognized the very childish and immature handwriting, to say nothing of the phraseology, yet he wrote back as gravely as though the letter had been a document of state:

"No doubt all you say is true, so far as you can know facts. But in this life facts must be taken into consideration and, for the present, I am more content to be a large leading man than a small part of the glow from the milky way."

The foregoing is mentioned simply to illustrate a certain side of Mr. Bennett's character. He addressed his own children as gravely as he had

(Continued on page 121)

Photograph by Hurrell

Constance Bennett's first marriage was to Chester Moorehead, a student at the University of Virginia. He escorted her to a number of football games and proms—and there was a runaway marriage. Miss Bennett's parents promptly had the marriage annuled.

The Romance of the Comet Girl

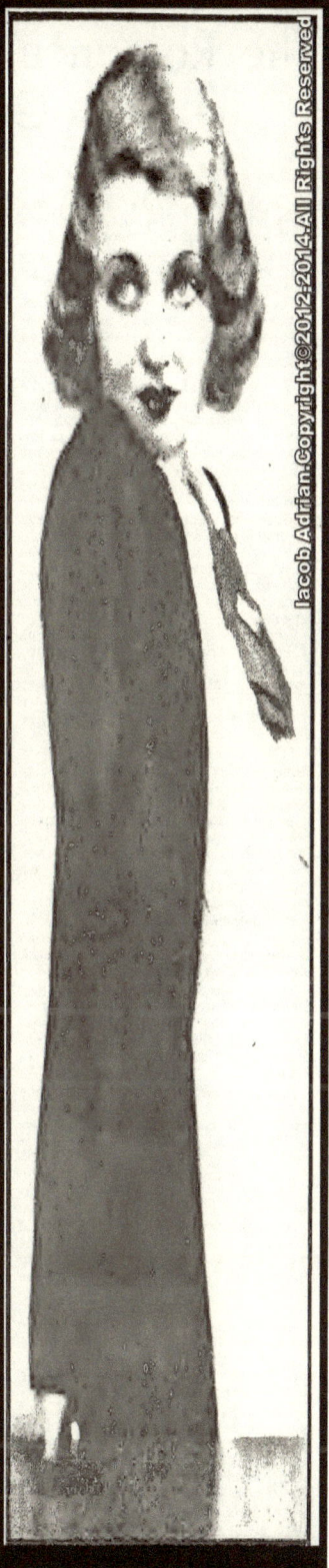

Jacob Adrian Copyright©2012-2014-All Rights Reserved

me. He talked to them as though they were grown. Is it any wonder in such an environment that Constance should have matured early? Should have become the poised and logical young lady she now is?

If she could talk to her parents and show them that what she wanted was best for her—or at least as good as what they wanted her to do—she usually had her way.

MRS. BENNETT comes from a long line of distinguished theatrical people. Her father was Lewis Morrison, who played Mephistopheles in "Faust" for seventeen years. Her mother was Rose Wood, once Lester Wallack's leading lady and later a member of the Philadelphia stock company which featured Georgie Drew and Maurice Barrymore. She has always been exceedingly level-headed and it is from her Constance inherits her logic. Upon divorcing Richard Bennett, she abandoned the stage and started a play brokerage office.

But, at the time, Mrs. Bennett was more concerned with her children than with her career or plays. She had seen too much of the seamy side of professional life to want her daughters launched in it. She tried to foster an interest in them in the things that occupied other children.

But Mr. Bennett was continually inviting theatrical people to the house—successful men—and he, being what he was—and is—was continually arguing with them. Constance would slip quietly into the room and sit unobtrusively in the corner, absorbing it all. Sometimes a glint of amusement would creep into her eyes over the vehemence of the debaters concerning some relitively unimportant matter, but she never interrupted.

And after she had been there for ten or fifteen minutes her mother would discover her presence and send her out to play.

When she was about five Mr. Bennett decided that, stage or no stage, he was going to have a home life. And home to him meant having his family with him. In those days he devoted a season to playing in New York and the following season to touring—five or six months in Chicago, a few months in Boston and a couple of months in Philadelphia.

CONNIE grins today when she thinks of the entourage that used to set out with her father. In addition to her parents, her two sisters and herself, there were always both a French and a German governess, a valet for her father and a personal maid for her mother, besides the household servants to be engaged on their arrival in a city. Usually the valet, one of the governesses and her mother's maid traveled on the train but Mr. and Mrs. Bennett, the three children and the

other governess made the cross-country trek in a huge Locomobile—Mr. and Mrs. up front (he at the wheel in a large linen duster), the three children, the governess, the dogs and the gold-fish in the back—for the children would never leave their pets.

Once Connie was holding the goldfish bowl and decided the fish could not breathe with the lid screwed down tightly the way it was to keep the water in. She unscrewed the lid and surreptitiously threw it out the side of the car. Immediately the water started sloshing out of the bowl and presently a fish or two sloshed with it. One of the other children started to cry and Mr. Bennett looking around and seeing what had happened, brought the car to an abrupt stop, put the fish back in the bowl, marched up to the door of a farm house and made the farmer's wife a present of the aquarium. Connie wept copiously during the rest of the trip.

I asked what had caused the incident to stick in her mind.

"Why," she answered, "it was my first experience of the kind. If it had been one of the dogs he would have run after us and tried to get back to me but the fish just stayed at the farm. And it taught me that it's simply no good pinning your affections on a fish."

WHEN she was about ten they took a place in New York and for the first time in her life Connie began attending day school. Her education theretofore had been gotten from private tutors. Later she attended Miss Chapin's School, Miss Shandor's on Park Avenue and still later Miss Merrill's Finishing School. She lived at the latter place during her year there.

One afternoon a week she was permitted to attend teas, providing her home work didn't suffer as a result and provided she was properly chaperoned. She has always had a phenomenally retentive memory. Even now, she reports for rehearsals two days later than the balance of the company because she is always the first up in her lines.

Well, in those dear, dead days Connie's home work was a joke. She would read a lesson over once or twice and it stuck with her. She never had to "cram" for an examination. So she and her chaperone went cookie pushing every afternoon instead of the allotted once a week.

At the end of the term, with one of the highest averages in the school, Mrs. Bennett was dumbfounded when the principal said very sweetly, "I'd prefer, Mrs. Bennett, if you would send Constance somewhere else next year. I don't mean that she isn't a good student, because she is, but she's an unsatisfactory student. You see, she learns easily so it doesn't interfere with

The Romance of the Comet Girl

Jacob Adrian.Copyright©2012-2014.All Rights Reserved

her school work if she goes to teas every afternoon. But other students don't learn so easily. They hear Constance talk of the good times she has had, so they, too, perforce, must go tea-ing, and *their* work *does* suffer."

You see, even in those days Constance had her own way at no sacrifice on her part. Life sort of gravitated about her.

BY this time she had begun to take part in the discussions of her father and his friends. Always a keen observer and an omnivorous reader, Connie was well posted on the theater and personalities connected with it, even though the stage itself held no attraction for her. Her mother, partly because she wanted Constance to have the finish a European education would give her, and partly because she was afraid Connie might become infected with the germ *theatricalis*, took her to Paris and put her in Mme. Balsan's school.

So far so good. Connie had visions of herself strolling down the Champs Elysees or the banks of the Seine with some distinguished looking foreigner or some boy from home studying literature or art. But French schools are not like that.

"The average American going to Paris to school is apt to have a pretty rude awakening when she gets there," Constance smiled. "You're guarded like a prisoner in a jail and chaperoned like—like—*you* think up a good simile," she finished. "When we were allowed out (and it was seldom enough) we went *en masse* and with almost as many chaperones as there were pupils."

Her determination and logic are illustrated by the fact that she talked her parents out of sending her back there for a second term.

Sixteen and her schooling behind her. The next Winter she was formally presented to the society of diplomatic circles in Washington by an uncle connected with the American Embassy in Peking.

It was during this period that she developed her reputation as a prom trotter and became a familiar figure at the dances of all the Eastern universities.

Connie has been called cold, hard, predatory—a lot of other unpleasant things.

As a matter of fact, she is none of the things she has been called and the fact that a man was interested in another girl would not even arouse passing interest in Connie. Men gravitate towards her as—to use a trite expression—moths to a flame. The flame doesn't dim its glow to keep from burning the moths. Neither can Constance dim her charm to prevent men falling in love with her.

The only thing I can think of that would make her seem less than irresistible is a lack of interest in a person. If a person fails to attract her, an air of boredom that she can neither fight nor escape envelops her like a mantle.

And it is these disgruntled folk who have given her the reputation of being "ritzy", "high-hat", this, that and the other thing. A person knowing her is startled at the warmth and humor lurking beneath her calm, detached exterior.

THE boys met at the dances and teas were simply diversion until she met Chester Moorehead, a student at the University of Virginia. He escorted her to a number of football games and proms and she discovered there was "that certain something" about him. The next thing we knew he had persuaded the reckless Constance to elope with him.

A creature of impulses, I could never conceive of her marrying in any other way than by eloping. Not because she would be afraid of opposition but because anything vital she did would be on the spur of the moment. If she announced her engagement and planned a church wedding, by the time the wedding day rolled around she would probably be in love with someone else—or at least no longer in love with the man to whom she had been engaged.

But for once Connie couldn't have her way and her parents had her marriage annulled. They were adamant on that point. The legal end of it out of the way, the whole family—including Connie—sailed for Europe.

On her return, she found the empty round of teas, bridge and dances failed to satisfy and no longer interested her. She began to study drawing—covers and sketches of the *Vogue* and *Vanity Fair* type. In the back of her mind was the idea that she would eventually open a modiste shop in this country and design the gowns herself.

Unknown, even to herself, at the time, Constance had said goodbye to domesticity. She was launched—definitely—upon a career!

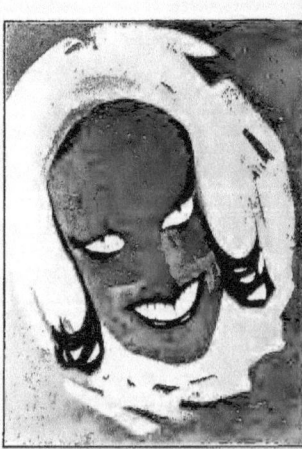

Joan Crawford, as seen by Coke, the well-known Latin-American caricaturist, who spares no one.

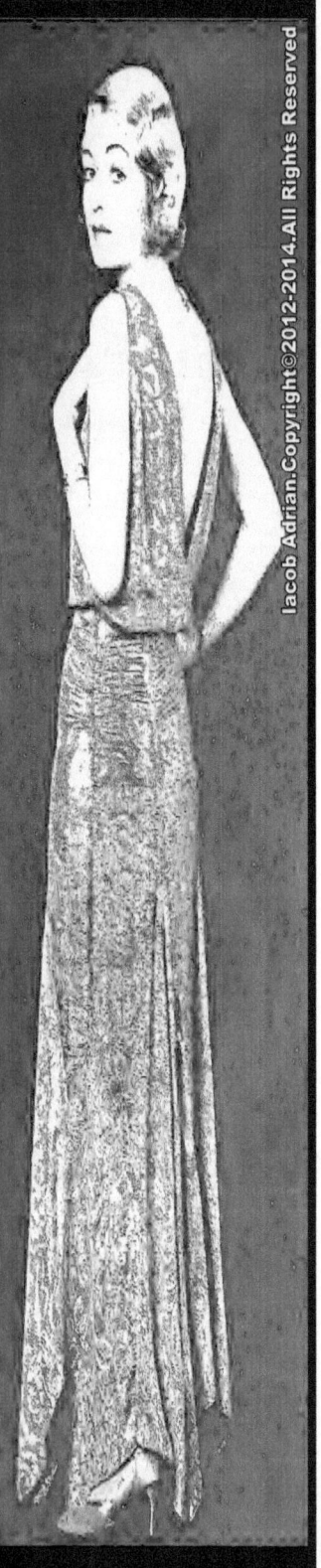

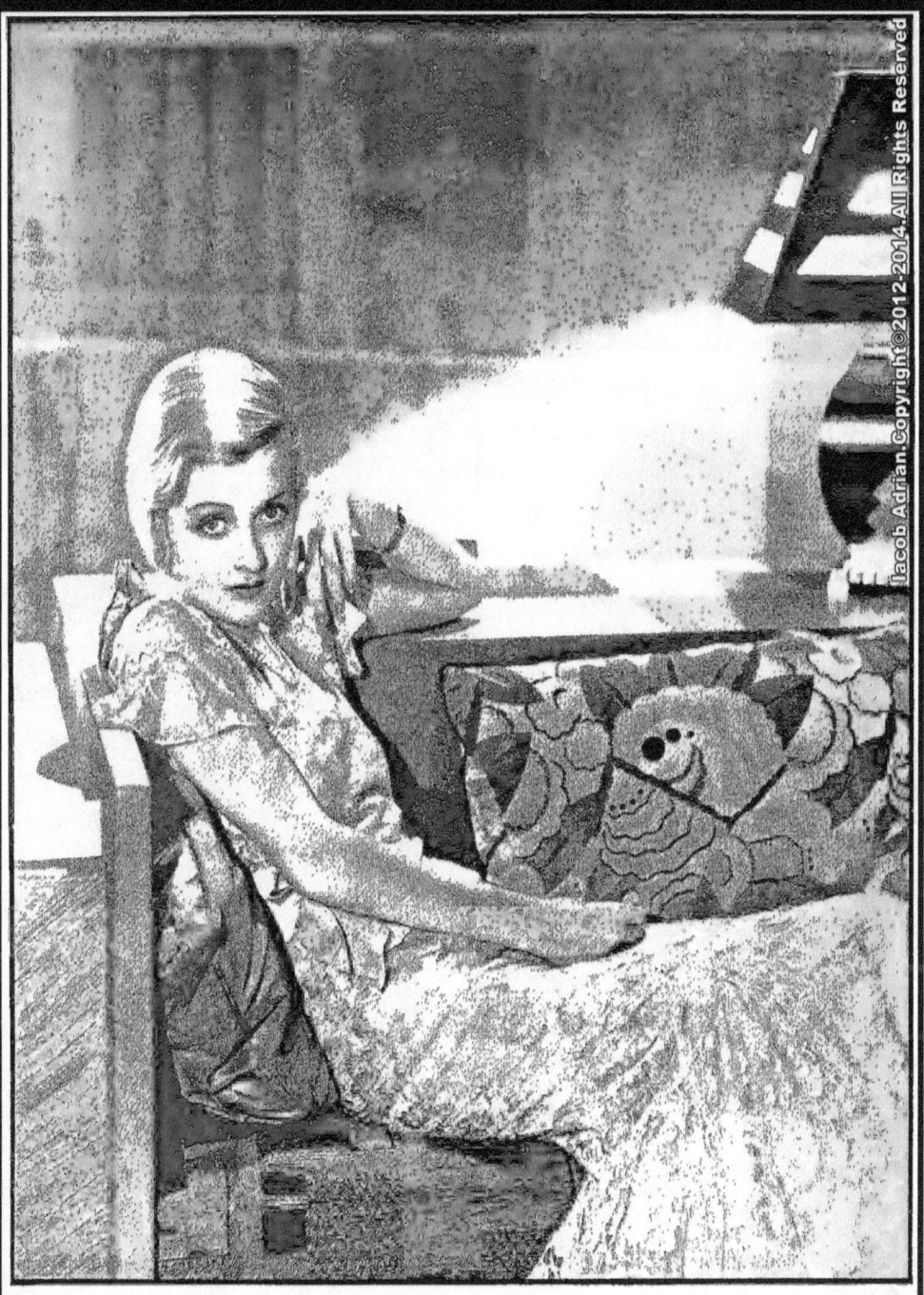

Jacob Adrian Copyright ©2012-2014 All Rights Reserved

Constance Bennett entered motion pictures over the objections of her parents, particularly her father, Richard Bennett, the stage star. She was but seventeen when she tried her luck first. Her success was immediate and surprising—but she tossed it all aside to marry Philip Plant. Love is like that. "If I fell in love today—and the man wanted me to leave pictures, I'd do it without a moment's hesitation," Miss Bennett admits. "If I married outside my profession, I'm not sure I wouldn't want to give it all up again. The chances for happiness would be greater."

The Romance of the COMET GIRL

How Love and a Career Fought for Supremacy in Constance Bennett's Life

By S. R. MOOK

CONSTANCE BENNETT'S picturesque career touches its high points in New York, Paris and Hollywood.

Last month NEW MOVIE told how both her father and mother came of distinguished stage families. Her father is Richard Bennett, the footlight star. Her mother is Adrienne Morrison, whose father, Lewis Morrison, was a celebrated stage star of his day.

Miss Bennett, with her sisters, Joan and Barbara, was raised in the ever changing household of a theatrical family. As she grew up, Constance Bennett attended several New York finishing schools. She was sent to Mrs. Balsan's School in Paris and—at sixteen—was presented to society in Washington.

The Bennetts planned to keep Constance from a stage career. Miss Bennett became a familiar figure at college proms—and she met Chester Moorehead, a student at the University of Virginia. There was a runaway marriage—but her family had the ceremony annulled. Constance was sent to Europe to forget. She took up drawing and planned to follow art and designing as a career.

PART II

IT was about this time Constance Bennett met Philip Plant. She was going up to New Haven to a football game and dance with a friend and young Plant drove up with them. He fell and fell hard.

His mother was married for the third time to the then District Attorney of New York—Colonel Hayward, the father of Leland Hayward. And Leland, in turn, was married to Connie's best friend, Lola Gibbs. So Mr. Plant had things pretty much his own way. He became extremely intimate with his stepbrother and wife and was constantly suggesting that Mrs. Hayward invite Constance Bennett to join them on a party.

Two or three months of that and he and Constance were engaged. It was shortly after Mr. Plant had been in an automobile accident and involved in an unpleasant suit for damages.

MR. BENNETT was no more enthused over his daughter's engagement to Mr. Plant than he had been over her marriage to Mr. Moorehead. So the family proceeded to Europe a second time.

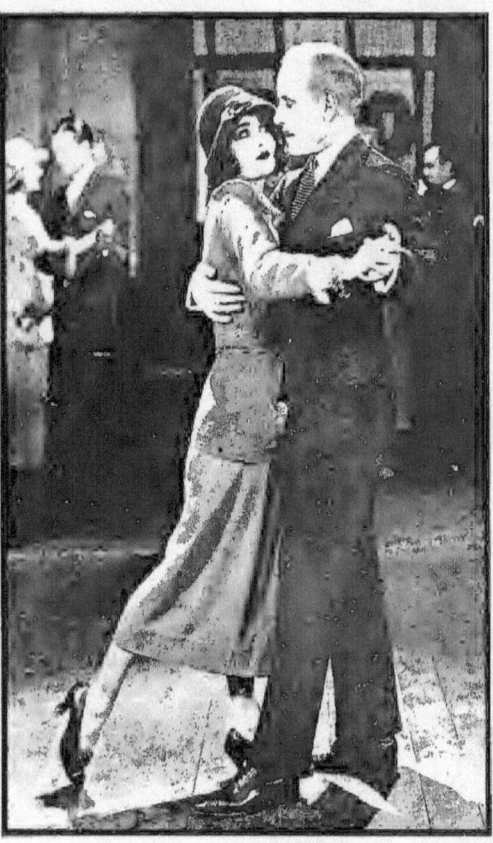

Back in 1924 Constance Bennett had a brief—but flashing—taste of screen success. One of her hits at that time was scored in "Cytherea." She is shown above in a scene from that film with Lewis Stone.

But young Mr. Plant was in earnest and promptly followed them. In Europe he succeeded in convincing Mr. Bennett of his eligibility and the engagement was announced, with plans for an October wedding. Obstacles and objections having been removed, Constance returned to this country with her parents. She and her fiancé immediately began to make themselves miserable by quarreling and the engagement was broken.

Partly to forget and partly as a gesture towards independence, she accepted an offer to play the lead opposite her father in "The Dancers."

Her first engagement the lead in a Broadway production opposite a famous star! Much it mattered to Connie. She found out she would have to sign a "run

How Constance Bennett Gave Up SUCCESS for LOVE

of the play" contract which meant that she must continue with the show as long as it was in New York and then go on tour with it indefinitely—or until her father tired of it and the producers shelved it. Connie declined to leave New York. Intuitively she knew that the romance between herself and Philip Plant was not ended — nowhere near it and she wanted to remain in New York.

Then another engagement was offered her. She accepted it and walked out of the cast while the play was still in rehearsal. The leading man had insisted upon making love to her when they weren't rehearsing. "I didn't object to being made love to," she explained, "I merely objected to being made love to by *that* man."

IT was about this time she attended the Equity Ball with her father. Samuel Goldwyn was there. There has never been anything the matter with Sam's eyesight and Connie's beauty seared him

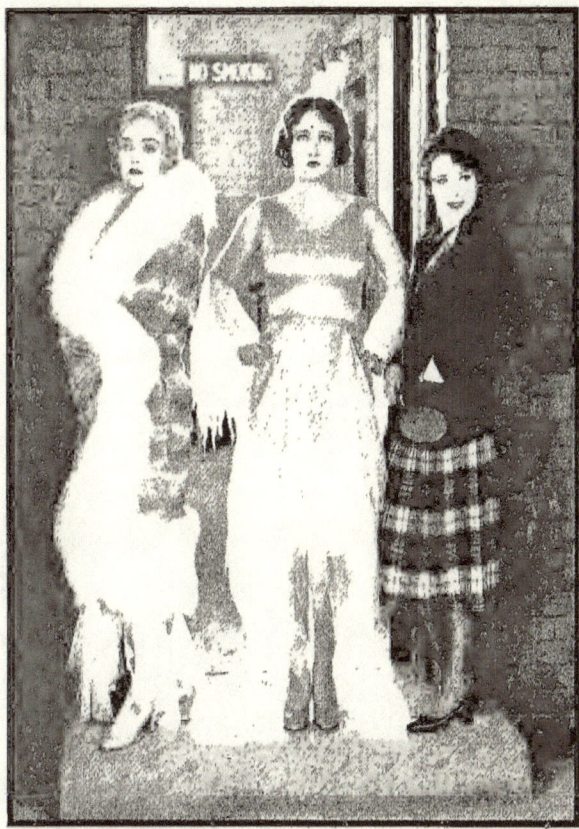

One of Constance Bennett's early hits was made in "Sally, Irene and Mary." This, oddly enough, also marked one of Joan Crawford's earliest big hits. At that time Sally O'Neil, the third of the trio, was looked upon as one of the most promising of the younger screen actresses. Left to right: Misses Bennett, Crawford and O'Neil.

ened and finally had her way after promising faithfully that she would return as soon as the picture was finished and not ask to stay on the West Coast alone. She wanted to get away from New York— away from Phil Plant and everything that reminded her of him.

JUST before she left New York Paramount made a test of her and wanted to sign her on a contract to start when she finished "Cytherea." Her father was all for signing. "Oh, no," said the logical Constance. "They wouldn't want me at that figure unless they were satisfied I was going to be good. If I'm good they'll make a lot of money on me. Well, I say if I'm good, I'll make the money myself. I'll take my chances freelancing."

She came West and made "Cytherea."

Plant phoned her by long distance, apologized and asked her to come back to New York. Connie hung up the phone. A short time later he phoned again, this

like a white flame. He offered her the lead in Joseph Hergesheimer's "Cytherea"—a best seller of that period.

Long arguments characterized the conversation in the Bennett household at that time. Mrs. Bennett was bitterly opposed to the idea of Constance entering pictures. Her father saw no harm in it.

Constance put an end to the discussions herself. "I'm seventeen now—almost eighteen. When I'm eighteen I'll be of age and free to do as I please. You can stop me now, but you'll only be postponing matters, because when I'm of age I'll go into pictures, anyhow. The only thing you'll do is knock me out of this opportunity."

Mrs. Bennett capitulated and Constance signed for the picture which was to be made in the East.

Then she and Philip Plant became reconciled and life took on a roseate glow again. But happiness, at best, is transitory and nothing lasts.

She and Plant quarreled again—violently this time, and the engagement was broken a second time.

As if to aggravate matters, Mr. Goldwyn decided to film "Cytherea" in Hollywood and Mrs. Bennett renewed her objections. This time it was Constance who was adamant. She wept, stormed, pleaded, cajoled, threat-

time that unless she came back he was going to marry someone else. "It's your privilege," said Constance, and added sweetly, "I certainly wish you happiness. Goodbye."

A few days later he phoned again to announce his engagement. The maid who was working for Connie almost wrecked the romance for keeps that time.

Connie, with a fiendish sense of humor and always with a flair for the unusual, had engaged a maid who was largely a mixture of Japanese and Irish, but in whom there was also a goodly portion of Scotch and West Indian—with a trace of Russian thrown in for good measure. If your imagination can encompass such a heterogeneous mixture, you may have some idea of what she looked like—to say nothing of her mentality.

Connie kept a small bungalow in Beverly Hills and this one maid, who was a general factotum. Her life in those days was one mad whirl. She used to go home at night so tired she could hardly drag one foot after the other. Throwing herself across the bed, she would tell the maid not to disturb her for an hour. The phone would ring and Mr. Blank would ask to speak to Connie. The maid would ask for his name and then carefully explain that

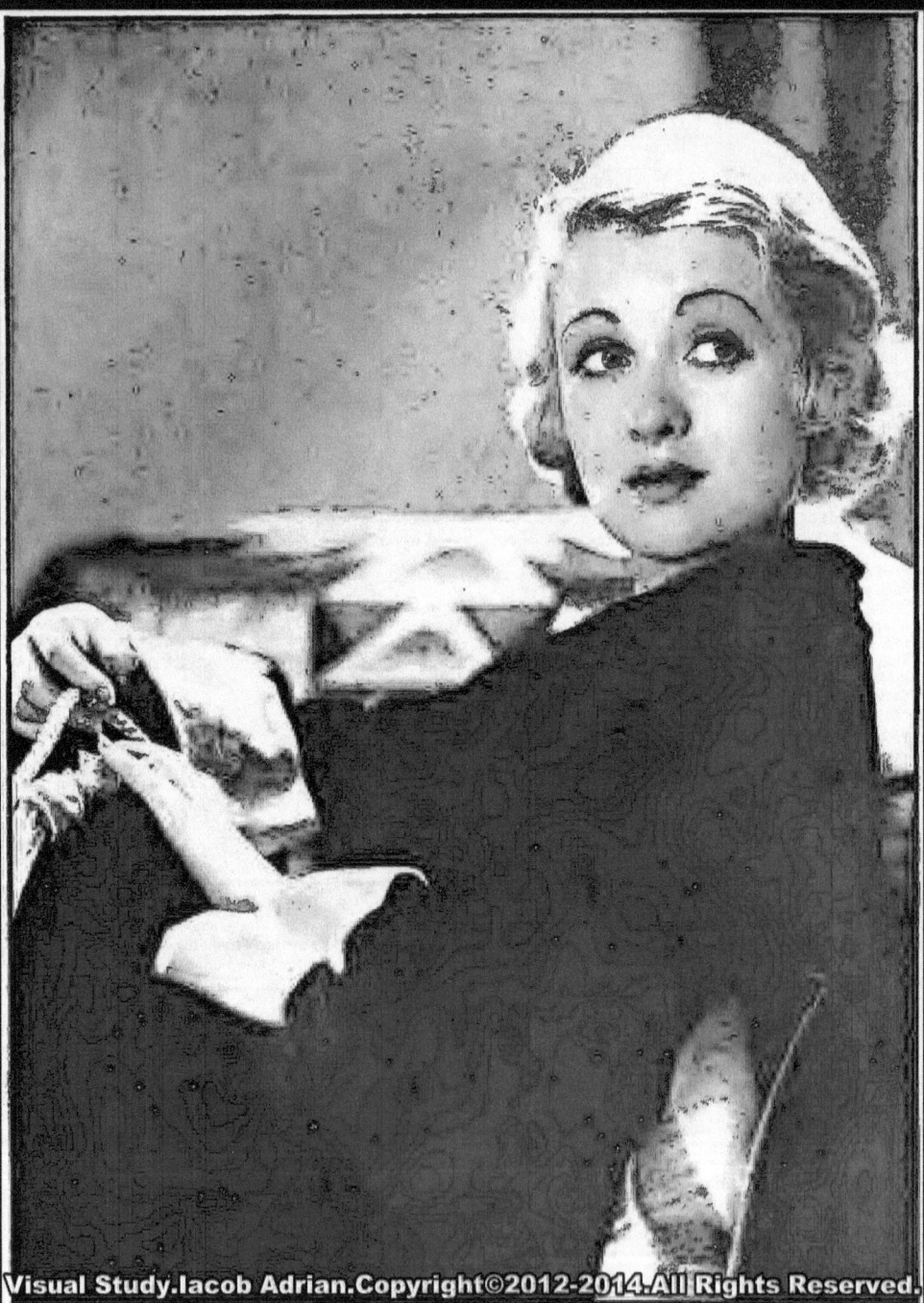

Visual Study.Iacob Adrian.Copyright©2012-2014.All Rights Reserved.

Constance Bennett's marriage to Philip Plant marks a romantic chapter in her life story. For several years they maintained a home in Paris, one on the Riviera and another at Cannes. They were familiar figures at Deauville and other famous watering places. Constance's salon became celebrated in Paris. Yet their romance grew cold. They tried desperately to make things right, but failed. Then Miss Bennett turned back to Hollywood.

Romance of The Comet Girl

Miss Bennett was resting and could not be disturbed for an hour. In half an hour or forty-five minutes, Mr. Blank's impatience getting the best of him, he would call again. The maid would ask who was calling and on getting Mr. Blank's name would fly into a rage that would have done credit to any one of the six nations whose blood coursed in her veins—to say nothing of the mixture. "You so-and-so," she would scream, "didn't I tell you she couldn't be disturbed?"

ONE of Mr. Plant's calls came during such a period. "Long distance" meant nothing in the life of this maid. She calmly told the operator Connie couldn't be disturbed. A short time later the operator rang again and the maid flew into one of her customary rages. Mr. Plant was already on the other end of the wire and, not hearing clearly or understanding the ungodly dialect the maid spoke, jumped to the conclusion that Connie was refusing to speak to him.

The telephone operator eventually put the call through and Constance received the momentous news of his engagement. She ought to make an excellent poker player. She can't be bluffed.

She went right on with the picture and presently it was finished. She returned to New York and the film was released—a smash hit and Connie was something of a sensation.

Then the offers began pouring in and she went back to the West Coast. She was out here nine months this time—and made nine pictures: "Into the Net," "Code of the West," "The Goose Hangs High," "My Son," "My Wife and I," "The Goose Woman," "Wandering Fires," "Marriage" and "Sally, Irene and Mary." It was in the last-named picture that Joan Crawford got her first real break and Sally O'Neil was also prominently among those present.

These pictures were all made as a free lance player and at a constantly mounting salary. Only those of you who can remember back five or six years ago can have any idea of the fan following and popularity she developed in those few months. After each picture she was deluged with new offers of contracts, but it was not until after "Sally, Irene and Mary" that M.-G.-M. finally talked her into affixing her signature to a contract. The document stated she was to have a six weeks' vacation every year. She started her new contract by taking the first year's vacation at the beginning instead of the end.

WHEN Plant saw that his newly announced engagement was having no effect on Constance, he broke it and came West himself. He arrived during the latter part of her stay.

Connie loved him. She had never tried to kid herself that she didn't. She has always had a good head and usually she keeps it clear. Young as she was, she realized that marriage is a serious business and she had tried to reason whether she and Plant could be happy together. It was when she decided they couldn't that she had broken the engagement.

When Plant came West, it seemed good to her to see him again after nine months and, when they sat down and chatted, the things they had quarreled about seemed trivial.

So they became engaged for the third time and made plans to be married in January. Then Constance signed her M.-G.-M. contract and they returned to the East together. She still had two pictures to make for another company which she had contracted to do before signing with M.-G.-M. One of them—the first—was to have been made in New York. But no sooner had she and Plant arrived there than the officials told her she would have to leave for Palm Beach.

Plant objected. They had been separated for nine months, had just become reconciled and now they would have to be separated again. "I don't want it that way," he pleaded. "Let's be married now. I've more money than we need and there's no sense to your working yourself to death this way."

CONNIE agreed. They were married in November. The head of the company for whom she was to make those two pictures gave her a release from her contract as a wedding present and M.-G.-M. waived the contract with the understanding that, if she ever returned to pictures, she would come back to them and finish it out.

Then, perversely enough, although Plant had objected to her going to Palm Beach to make a picture he took her there on their honeymoon.

People have tried to make much of the fact that Constance is selfish; yet, on her honeymoon, she did one of the most unselfish things I have ever encountered.

Barbara, her sister, had gotten herself into the headlines—quite accidentally—but the newspapers were making much of it. Connie received a wire from her father: "Barbara in trouble. I am appearing in a play and cannot leave. Will you go?"

And Connie wired back: "Tonight." She threw her things into some bags, cut short her honeymoon and left that night as she had promised, explaining to friends, "The papers are trying to put Barbara in a mess. I've got to go and straighten it out and bring her back."

She brought Barbara back to New York with her and then she and her husband left for Europe. They maintained a house in Paris, a home on the Riviera and another at Cannes, and the two became familiar figures at Biarritz, Deauville and the other famous watering places.

HER salon became quite celebrated. Visiting there, one almost invariably met the Who's Who of the French capital as well as celebrated and important visitors in town.

"How could you be satisfied without your career?" I asked Miss Bennett the other day.

Connie's blue eyes widened and she regarded me levelly: "My boy, if you ever fall as deeply in love as I was, you'll know that there is nothing in the world that matters so much as being with the person you love. No price you can pay is too high, if it brings you happiness. I don't regret it."

And yet there are those who have said her heart never rules her head!

"Right now," she continued, "I think I'm getting a lot more important breaks than I ever did before I married, yet if I fell in love today with a man and he wanted me to leave pictures, I'd do it without a moment's hesitation."

"I think a man would have to be pretty selfish to ask you to leave pictures now," I interjected.

She turned that over in her mind for a moment and regarded me with an amused expression. "Not at all. People who are not directly concerned with the making of pictures simply cannot understand the business. Your time isn't your own; you never know when you may have to break an engagement you had planned on for days simply to attend a conference of some sort at the studio. Neither can they understand why you have to establish social relations with people you work with in this business more than any other. If I married outside my profession, I'm not sure I wouldn't want to give it up again. I think the chances for happiness would be greater."

Her eyes took on a faraway look and it was easy to guess she was living over those years abroad again.

She and Plant were happy for a time —a rather long time as happiness goes —and then the old differences began cropping up again; the same things that had caused them to break their engagement twice before they married. They tried, but it was no use.

Four years had written "Finis" to the chapter in Connie's existence called "Marriage." She secured a divorce, picked up the broken skeins of her life and faced the future.

Next month the most colorful chapters of Miss Bennett's meteoric career will be told in NEW MOVIE. *This covers her return to the screen, following her divorce from Philip Plant. It relates her recent adventures in Hollywood and tells how she came to meet with her great film success.*

The NEW MOVIE MAGAZINE

10¢ IN U.S.
15 CENTS IN CANADA

THE LARGEST CIRCULATION OF ANY SCREEN MAGAZINE IN THE WORLD

JUNE 1931

Visual Study.Jacob Adrian.Copyright©2012-2014.All Rights Reserved.

CONSTANCE BENNETT

The **MORALS** of **HOLLYWOOD** by Judge Ben B. Lindsey

The **REAL STORY** of **MARLENE DIETRICH**

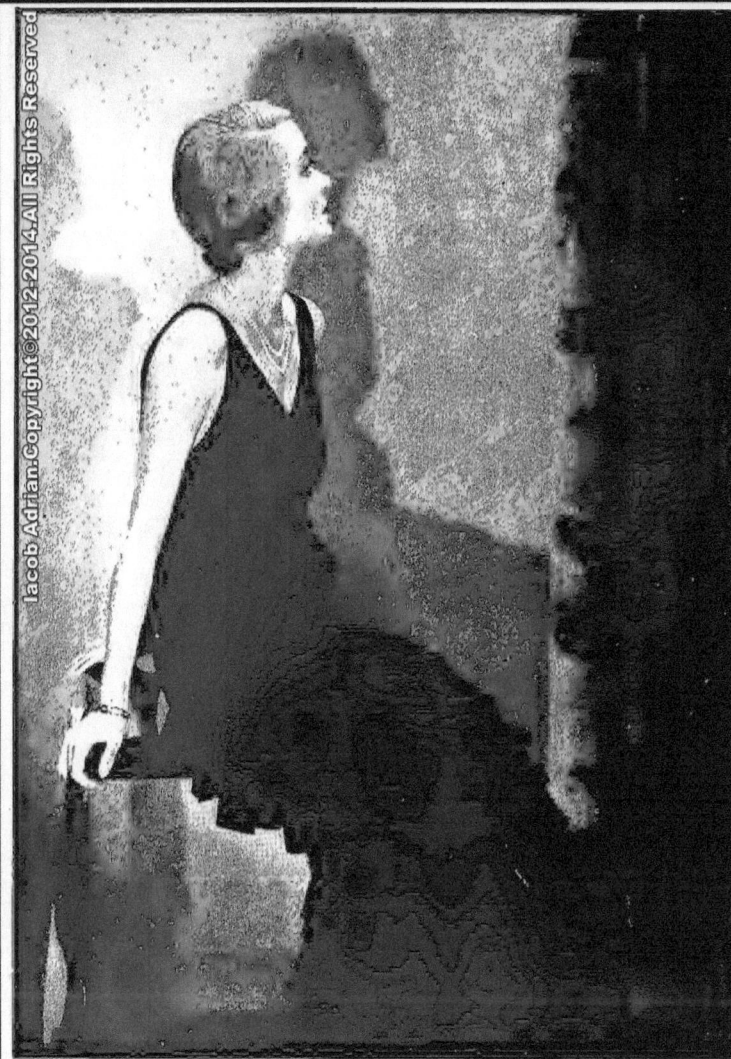

Jacob Adrian Copyright©2012-2014 All Rights Reserved

Constance Bennett is one of the most interesting figures in pictures today. Her poise and sophistication have singled her out for immediate recognition. She moves but little in movie circles. Her closest friends are not concerned with motion pictures. She is oddly aloof from rumors—and there are many of them—that revolve about her in the film colony.

of Pathé, heard she was considering a return to pictures. He immediately approached her. Connie had been on the verge of signing the Ufa contract at a large salary. She could make pictures in Europe, but in America there was that uncompleted contract with M.-G.-M.

NEGOTIATIONS hung fire for two weeks. Many were the long-distance calls put through across the Atlantic during that time. Conversations with Mr. Kennedy, with her attorney, with M.-G.-M. As soon as the last-named company had heard there was a chance of her coming back to the films they wanted her to finish out her contract.

That contract had been made at what seemed an exorbitant figure for her services, even in those days, but in the face of the sal-

PART III

THAT was in March, 1929. Coincidentally the talkies were just getting a firm foothold in the picture industry and the various companies were rushing about as haphazardly as ants, trying to secure new talent.

Connie's poise and sophistication, her beauty and the husky cadences of her voice were as famous in Europe as they have since become in America. The Ufa officials in Germany knew of her, knew of her theatrical ancestry and learned of her divorce. They also knew that there is no anodyne for sorrow equal to hard work, and they realized their chance had come. They sent a representative to see her, with instructions to sign her for two pictures.

Four years of shopping, of an empty round of social pleasures—teas and bridge in the afternoons; theaters, night clubs, bridge and dancing in the evenings—had begun to pall upon her. Besides, what was the use? She and Philip were estranged. She might better go back to pictures for a time.

She was on the point of signing with Ufa when the Marquis de la Falaise, who was acting as personal representative in Paris for Joseph F. Kennedy, then head

ary she had been offered by Pathé and Ufa (who were bidding against each other and constantly raising the ante) the M.-G.-M. remuneration looked like pin-money. Eventually M.-G.-M. gave Miss Bennett a release and let Pathé and Ufa fight out the battle between themselves. And Pathé finally got her.

It is interesting to note that M.-G.-M. recently paid Pathé $125,000 for Connie's services for one picture, "The Easiest Way."

But let Miss Bennett explain. "I signed for five years," she says. "I'd have signed for ten if they had asked me, because I had no intention of remaining in pictures. I thought I would come over, do one or two pictures and then retire again. But it sort of gets into your blood. You start going good and you work like the deuce to see if you can't go better."

Hardly had she signed her contract, closed her Paris house and boarded a liner than trouble commenced. Aboard the steamer she received a cablegram from the Pathé publicity department in New York:

"On your arrival you will be faced with battery of news cameramen and ship news reporters. A very clever young man in our department has thought up

The Romance of the
COMET GIRL

By S. R. MOOK

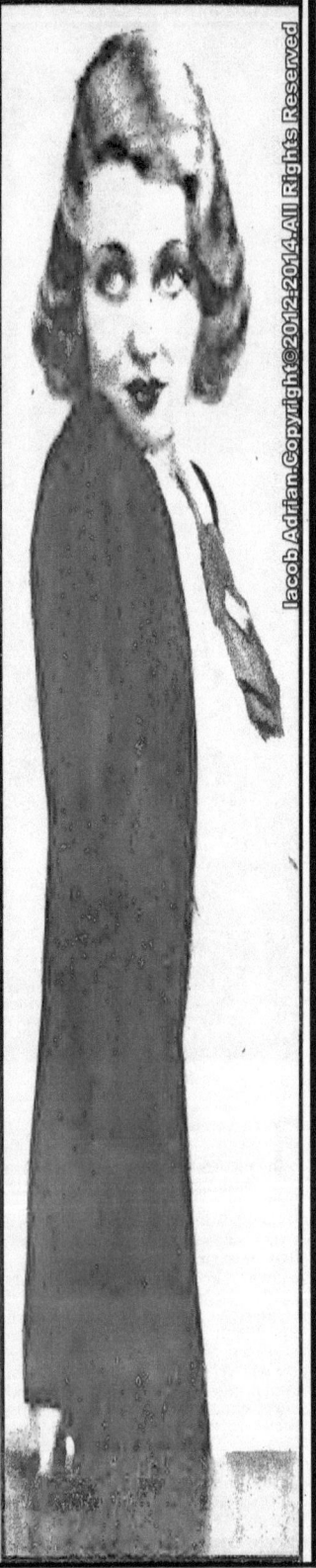

Jacob Adrian Copyright ©2012-2014 All Rights Reserved

splendid way for you to crash front pages in all papers. Idea is for you to say 'No young girl should ever marry a millionaire.' This may shock you at first, but am sure on thinking it over you will agree it is a clever idea."

Constance thought it over—for about two minutes—and sent this reply:

"Tell your clever young man that I don't want to crash the front pages in that way. For some inexplicable reason whenever I come to America I always land on the front pages—and without having to make an ass of myself to do it."

THAT was the beginning of her troubles. When she reached New York she related the incident to Mr. Kennedy, treated it as a joke and added, "Besides, why shouldn't a girl marry a millionaire if she wants to?"

And Mr. Kennedy repeated it as a joke. But, by the time it had gone the rounds, the humor had been deleted and it was told as a serious matter of big import. So immediately a young woman wrote an interview supposedly given out by Constance, called "Every Girl Should Marry a Millionaire."

"Now, how," Constance demanded in exasperation, "could every girl marry a millionaire? In the first place there aren't enough millionaires to go around and, in the second place, even if there were, it doesn't stand to reason that all of them would want to marry. It's ridiculous." But there was nothing that could be done about it.

Then came several other interviews which disturbed her—vexatious little things she was supposed to have said but hadn't—things that annoyed her in the same way a gnat or mosquito annoys a person. She began to resent interviewers who wrote what they pleased rather than what she said.

BUT the one that really infuriated Constance, and I have never seen her so burned up over anything, was one called "$250,000 a Year on Clothes!" "I never gave out any such interview," she stormed. "That girl came to me and began talking about clothes. I discussed them with her because I like clothes and I enjoy talking about them. But I never gave her the price of a single

AT this moment Constance Bennett is the most talked-about young actress in Hollywood. No player has made greater strides in popular favor during the past year.

Miss Bennett's childhood was typical of a theatrical family. Her father is Richard Bennett, the stage star, and her mother is Adrienne Morrison, herself an actress and the daughter of Lewis Morrison, a well-known stage star of his day. Miss Bennett attended smart schools in the East and in Paris and made her society début in Washington. About this time she met Chester Moorehead, student at the University of Virginia. There was a runaway marriage—but subsequently Miss Bennett was persuaded by her parents to go to Paris to forget.

Following her divorce and upon her return to America, she went into pictures. Her success was immediate, but she met Philip Plant, a young millionaire. After a hectic courtship, the two were married. Miss Bennett left the screen. Then followed four years spent abroad, in Paris and on the Riviera with her husband.

All this ended in another divorce and Miss Bennett picked up the broken skeins of her life and faced a new future. This month's instalment of her life story tells how she came to her present brilliant success and how she looks toward the future.

I happened to be on the set of "This Thing Called Love" the afternoon they finished shooting. The company was dismissed. Just as they started to leave the set the assistant director asked her to wait a moment. She turned and the director handed her a box containing two dozen American beauty roses which the electricians, prop men, camera men, grips and actors had chipped in to buy for her because it had been such a pleasant engagement and they had wanted to do something to fix it in her mind, too.

INCIDENTALLY, her personal maid has been with her for years. Her secretary, chauffeur, cook and housemaid are the same ones she engaged when she first returned to this country. Not a bad record for a star who is supposed to be selfish, cold-blooded and ritzy.

Her sense of humor is illustrated by another incident I witnessed. They were engaged upon a shot of Connie and her supposed-husband in a room together. "I'll turn on the radio," he announced.

"Don't bother," said Constance, "I'll do it."

"Ah, no," responded her husband, "I'll turn it on."

Nobody liked the way he read the last line but he himself. He rather fancied his inflections and stubbornly refused to change the delivery. The actor who played the husband is not without a sense of humor himself and, in talking about it afterwards, he laughed. "You can see," he said, "the line doesn't mean a damned thing. But I just happened to like the way I read it."

garment. I've always thought it was very poor taste to flaunt the price you pay for things—whether cheap or expensive—in people's faces. After I was gone, she went up to the publicity department of the studio and they filled in figures that are enough to start a revolution. A woman couldn't spend that much on clothes in a year."

The result of all this has been that Constance has refused to see writers, and this, in turn, has led to charges of "temperament."

Maybe she is temperamental, but I don't think so. I've known her for a long time and I've never seen any evidences of it. She has too keen a sense of humor for that sort of thing. If she ever did start throwing things, I imagine she would burst out laughing in the midst of it.

The Movie Meteor Flashing Across Hollywood

and all that sort of thing. The stage itself has never had any attraction for me and the fascination of a bare stage and the glamour of an empty auditorium is all a lot of hooey as far as I'm concerned. I much prefer pictures."

FOR those of you who must have FACTS: she is five feet four inches tall, usually weighs around ninety-eight pounds, has blond hair, fair skin and blue eyes. She had a Cadillac 16 roadster which she drove herself and rented a closed car when she wanted to go out at night. Recently she traded in the roadster on a convertible cabriolet so she could drive herself in the daytime and have her own chauffeur drive her at night.

She goes from one picture to another

with hardly an interim between them and, since her return to the screen, has made successively: "Rich People," "This Thing Called Love," "Son of the Gods," Three Faces East," "Common Clay," "Sin Takes a Holiday" and "The Easiest Way."

She goes her way, apparently untouched by and unconcerned over the rumors which fly about her. If something uncomplimentary reaches her and she thinks there is a foundation for it, she studies it over. If she thinks it is prompted by jealousy or envy, she ignores it.

Her closest friends are, for the most part, people not directly concerned with the motion picture industry.

And those who really know her cannot talk about her without raving. Don't I know? I'm one of them!

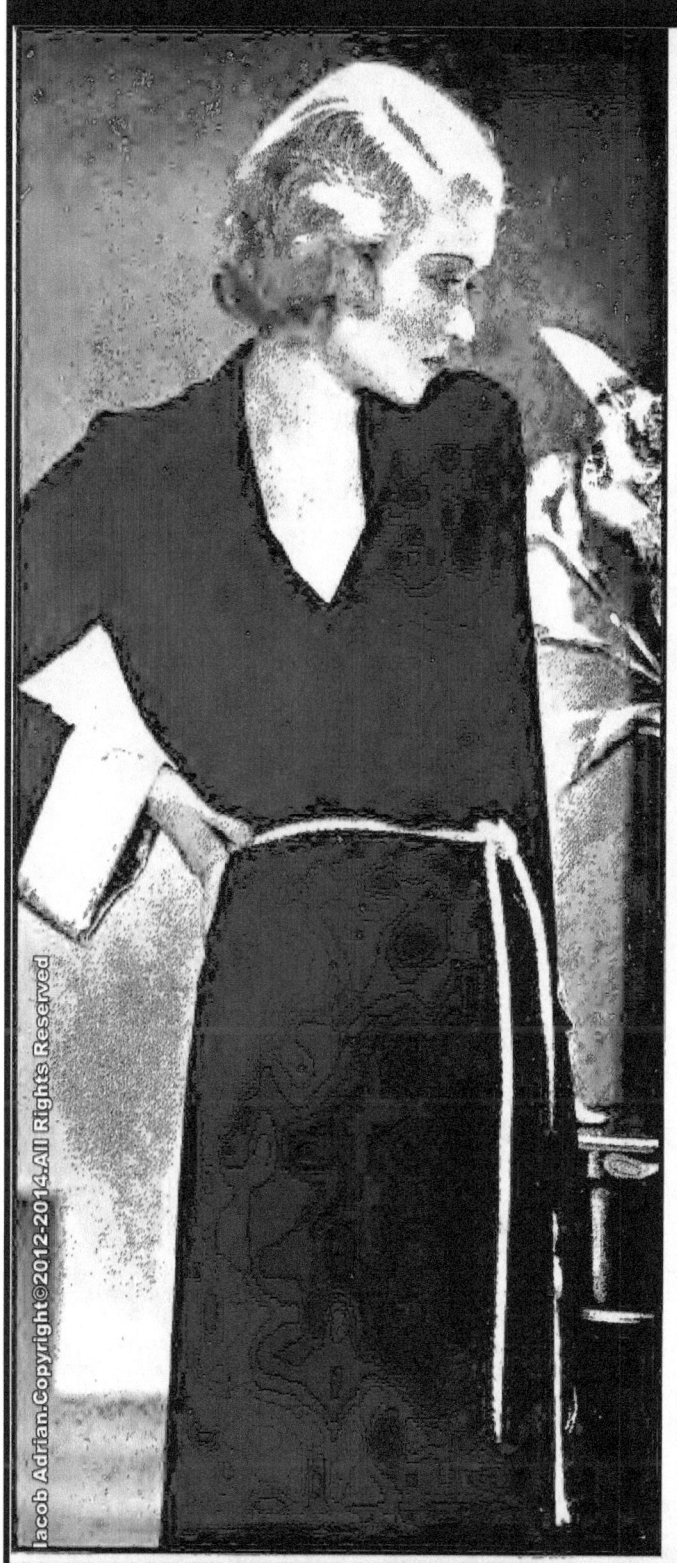

Iacob Adrian Copyright©2012-2014 All Rights Reserved

When Miss Bennett came back to pictures in 1929 she intended to make one or two films—and then quit again. "But it sort of gets into your blood," she admits. "You start going good and you work like the deuce to see if you can't go better."

The director was beside himself. Connie pulled him aside. "Don't worry. Just go ahead and take the shot. It'll be all right."

So they started the scene with the actor all puffed up and thinking he had won his point.

"I'll turn on the radio," he announced presently.

"All right," said Constance quite unconcernedly, thus removing all opportunity for him to deliver his last line. Being a good actor, he recovered himself quickly and the surprise he felt over the retort he got instead of the correct cue didn't show in his face.

TO me, Constance Bennett is the most interesting figure in pictures today. She may not have an angel's disposition. Few of us have, and as a rule those few are uninteresting to the point of deadliness.

But when she is upset over a thing or doesn't like a person, that person knows it. She doesn't say one thing to your face and another when your back's turned. Not so long ago she had an argument about her contract with Neil McCarthy, the Pathé attorney. The session lasted for hours. When it was finished Mr. McCarthy picked up the phone and called the studio executives, who were waiting to hear the outcome. "Whatever that girl says is O. K.," Mr. McCarthy announced. "She hasn't a crooked bone in her body, and when she fights, she fights in the open."

She has a clause in her contract that permits her to take ten weeks' vacation a year—all at one time, so she can go to Europe if she chooses. Last year she made the trip. This year she has forfeited the vacation in order to get in another picture or two.

"I can't understand," I said, "why you don't use those ten weeks to do a stage play."

"I'd die of fright if I ever had to face an audience across the footlights," she responded.

"But I should think the urge would be in your blood," I persisted. "Didn't you like to go back-stage when you were a kid and your father was a star?"

"Oh, sure," she answered carelessly, "but that was because I was the daughter of the star, and I could go sailing in while other people had to wait to be announced

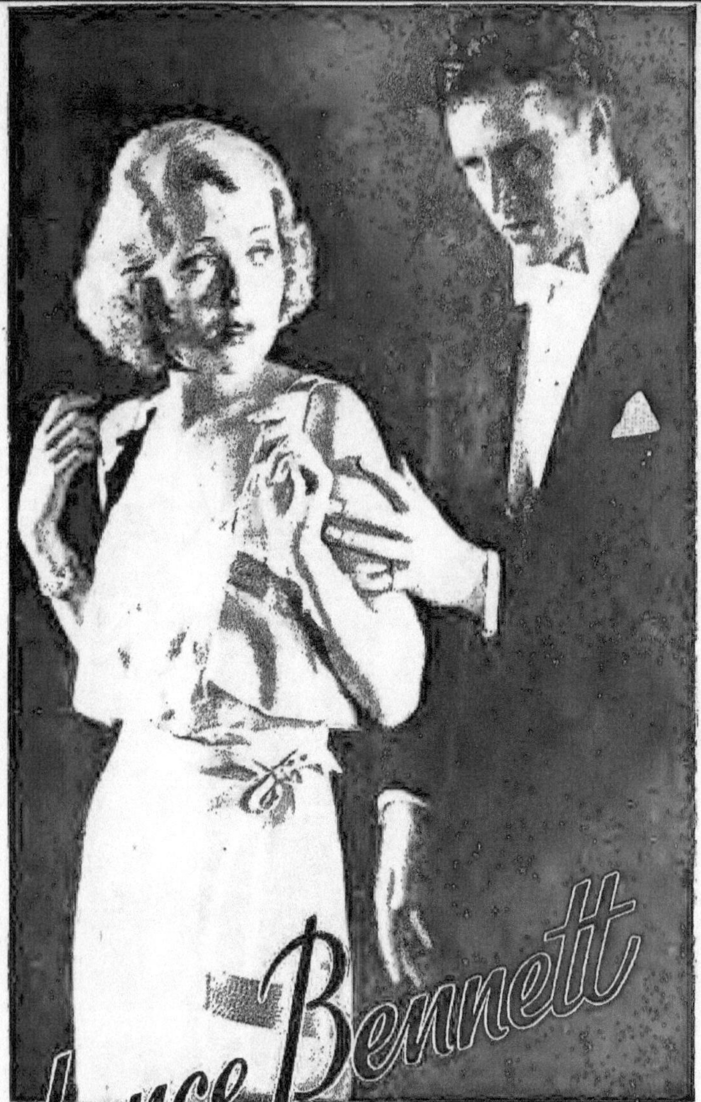

Iacob Adrian Copyright ©2012-2014 All Rights Reserved

Sold!

"Love would have been such an honest reason.. But you sold yourself."

WARNER BROS. presents:

Constance Bennett

in BOUGHT

A beautiful girl who takes but never gives!...loved but not loving! ...engaged but not married!...bought but not paid for!... *JACKDAWS STRUT* from which this great production comes has created more talk than any other novel of modern life...And Constance Bennett more gorgeously gowned—more emotionally satisfying—more dramatically supreme—makes it the finest picture play of her career...Directed by ARCHIE MAYO.

"Vitaphone" is the registered trademark of The Vitaphone Corporation

A WARNER BROS. & VITAPHONE PICTURE

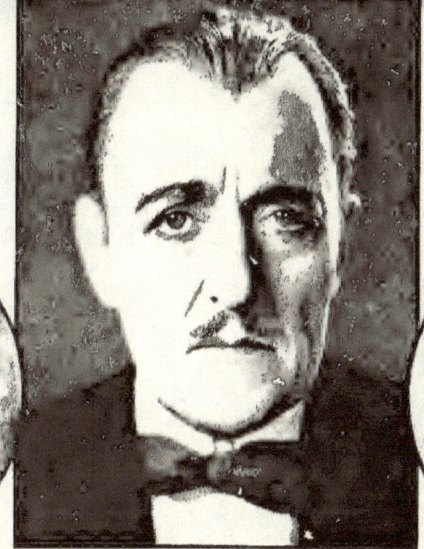

"Girls are not so very much different from boys; you can reason with them just so far and then—the spur. Theatrical managers have to be treated the same way.

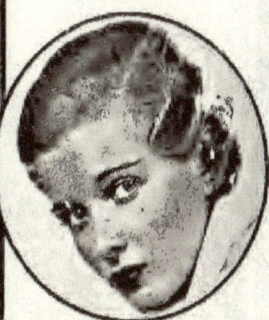

In the center is Richard Bennett; at the left, Constance, and, at the right, Joan. Years of theatrical tradition lie behind the success of the Bennett girls.

The Business of Being a FATHER

How Would You Like to be the Dad of Three Famous Daughters? Here's Richard Bennett's Story of How He Raised Them to be Stars

BY IVAN ST. JOHNS

SUPPOSE you were the father of those three little Princesses of Pictures, Constance, Joan and Barbara Bennett?

How would you treat them in these days of the full flare of their public favor?

How would you advise them about their finances and fiancés, their frivolities, if any, and their futures?

How would you have brought them up?

"IF they didn't do as they were told, I smacked 'em by depriving them of something they very much desired." Such was the answer given the last of these questions by their father, Richard Bennett, who, to carry on the metaphor of royalty, is by way of being a reigning prince in the realm of the theater and fast coming into exalted rank in the domain of sound on celluloid.

It is questionable as to the number of times Father Bennett ever smacked down Daughters Constance, Barbara and Joan, that much was obvious from the sardonic twinkle in his eye when he answered. They have always lived by the golden rule. Vesper bells will melt our greatest passions. But those who have known Richard Bennett in the theater and have seen the force he has put behind his efforts to accomplish things worth while will tell you that he most certainly must have "smacked 'em." The smacks were physical in his sense and maybe that was more effective, for he can and has delivered in another way the most thorough verbal smackings in a world where satire and sarcasm are keen and deadly weapons. As effective as smacks of the old and venerable woodshed variety.

"Girls are not so very much different from boys," he said, "as far as the matter of bringing up. You can reason with them just so far and then—the spur." No matter how ominous that pause, the threat of it was somewhat lessened by his smile. "I've known a lot of theatrical managers I had to treat the same way . . . only children have more sense as a rule."

"Do you think girls are too pampered?"

"Certainly—by fathers. Mothers handle them better; they know the chicanery of their sex."

And he said this notwithstanding the fact that his three daughters were sent to the finest schools in this country and in France.

"A diamond looks and is as little worth while as the devil was until polished." He said this with a very human and comforting degree of old-fashioned paternal pride which is more than justified, considering the results of that polishing.

MR. BENNETT'S oldest daughter is Constance. Miss Merrill's School at Mamaroneck and

"There's only one thing I ever tell my girls: don't do anything that is cheap, anything that must be explained to your real friends."—Bennett's advice to his girls.

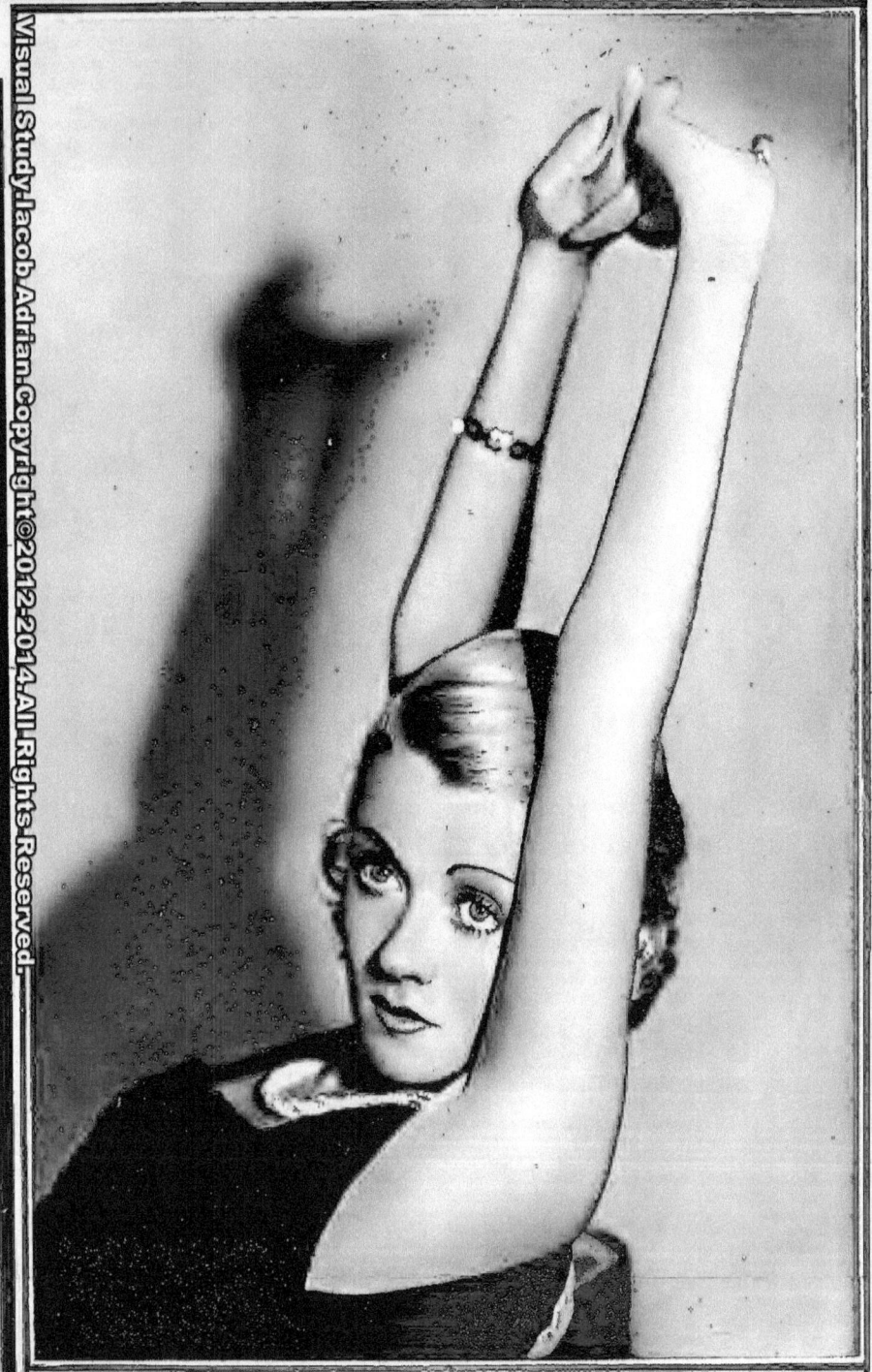

Visual.Study.Jacob.Adrian.Copyright©2012-2014.All.Rights.Reserved.

Richard Bennett's oldest daughter, Constance. She was sent to finishing schools in Mamaroneck, New York and Paris, and then made her social debut in Washington. All this was in preparation for a dramatic career—but neither Mr. Bennett nor his daughter knew it. Constance expected to make a happy and successful marriage—and then to lead a placid social life.

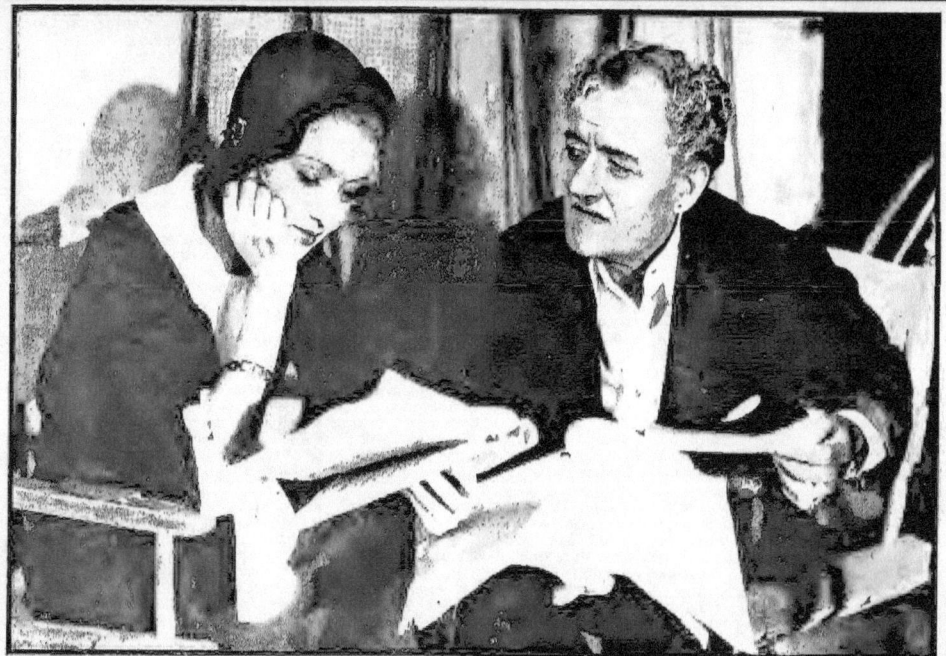

Constance Bennett and her famous daddy, Richard Bennett, between scenes of "Bought," in which both appear. For the first time, Mr. Bennett tells NEW MOVIE readers in this issue just what it means to be the father of three famous girls.

The Business of Being a Father

Miss Shandor's school on Park Avenue, Manhattan, took this first little Bennett diamond and processed her up, or down, to about a hundred and three pounds of loveliness. Then she was sent to Paris to acquire the final polish at the school of Mme. Balsan.

I imagine one of Dick Bennett's poorest pieces of acting was this attempt to appear casual about his first-born's success in New York, Washington and Baltimore society. He has been making a pretty poor job of his nonchalance ever since then. Try as he may he cannot hide his pride in what she has done . . . her début into the celluloid circle in "Cytherea" and her steady climb from that point to her present heady heights . . . a Pathe star, with enough of the Bennett brains and Morrison charm behind her beauty to hold her there.

In a minute we will get to what he has to say about his eldest's matrimonial gamble with young Phil Plant, sole heir to many Standard Oil millions.

Hardly was Constance well into the polishing stage than another small diamond appeared and Mr. and Mrs. Bennett called her Joan. Here was another daughter to be sent to school. To St. Margaret's at Waterbury, Conn., she went and thence to L'Ermitage, at Versailles, just outside of Paris. And here was another daughter returning with her polish about whom he had to appear casual. It was getting to be a strain.

Miss Joan started out along the social highway. She did not get very far. The heritage of Bennett claimed her

one day when she was watching her father rehearse in Jim Tully's play, "Jarnegan." Aside from being a writer and, if we believe his books, an ex-hobo, ex-bartender, ex-prize-fighter, and ex-examiner of Jack Gilbert, Jim Tully is by way of being an excellent judge of precious stones. He caught the gleam of the second Bennett diamond and made loud and raucous Tullyesque noises until Joan was given the ingénue part in her father's play.

DURING rehearsals would have been a grand opportunity for her father to have smacked her for not doing as she was told. Father Bennett has a way of smacking folks in his productions, with icy verbiage, mind you, and it generally results in better performance.

He must have smacked Joan plenty during these rehearsals, for she was a sensation . . . and Dick had to begin all over again posing as the bored and casual male parent.

Meanwhile, as if he wasn't groggy from portraying such an alien rôle for the benefit of Constance and little Miss Joan, a taller and dark jewel had come along. She is Barbara, the second daughter, who had preceded Joan through the fashionable Eastern finishing schools and the sojourn in France. Barbara showed her strain of the breed with her father in "The Dancers" in New York—then in "Syncopation," one of the first of the talking and singing pictures. She played opposite Morton Downey. You know

him, folks, Morton Downey, the Camel Minstrel boy? SURE!—Mr. Bennett was proud as punch of him.

He meant much more to Barbara than the family traditions. She had two sisters who would see to it that the name of Bennett remained on the marquees all over the country. So she married Morton and he conforms pretty perfectly to Richard Bennett's specifications for a husband.

"It's a cinch," he said, "to see that they have clothes and education. But it's much harder to see they have the love of real men in this day of phonies masquerading as such."

"Is that a father's business?" Of course that's a stupid question, and Mr. Bennett hates stupidity. It makes him flare up.

"That's his principal business." He was all father now, pacing up and down his living room at the Beverly Wilshire. "I talk it over with my girls . . . and if their men can pass this acid test . . . well, that's enough for me.

"HERE'S what I ask 'em. 'How far could this one or that one . . . whoever the chap may be . . . get without money? And how far would he really want to get? That's ambition. If the girls can satisfy themselves that the lad who is hovering around could get somewhere without an inherited bank roll behind him . . . then I say go to it . . . like that.'

"Like that," was accompanied by a snap of the fingers . . . a loud snap.

The Business of Being a Father

"One of the girls married a boy with too much money, but that wouldn't have made any difference, if he had only wanted to do something besides spend it."

Right here let the writers add that Morton Downey didn't have any money, but he's getting somewhere. Those two little songs every night bring him some $5,000 a week and cigarettes for the family.

"There's only one other thing I ever tell the girls," their father continued. "Don't do anything that is cheap. What I mean by cheap—anything that must be explained to your real friends."

And he went on to say that their breed has a certain luster and tradition for them to maintain. Adrienne Morrison is their mother and her roots are deep in the theater. Her mother, Rose Wood, went on the stage in New Orleans when she was eight years old. Her father—that would be the Bennett sisters' great-grandfather—was William Wood, famous old English pantomimist and the great-great-grandfather was manager of the ancient Drury Lane theater in London. Adrienne Morrison's mother, Rose Wood, became leading woman at the Wallack Stock Company in New York, when that city worshiped her along with Georgiana Drew, Lester Wallack and Rose and Charles Coghlan. There's a lineage for you on one side of a real family of the theater. Of course every old timer remembers their grandfather, Louis Morrison, confrere of Jefferson, James O'Neill, Mojeska, Booth, and Barrett.

FOR a father these three young women possess the subject of this interview. I remember very distinctly the occasion when Miss Maude Adams opened her season at the Empire Theatre in New York in James Barrie's play, "What Every Woman Knows." The canny Miss Adams had seen the play in London, where a celebrated star was playing the part of John Shand and enhancing his reputation thereby. Miss Adams felt her audiences came to see her and not her leading man, so she selected a comparatively unknown young man named Richard Bennett to play opposite her. She was wonderful in the play. . . . She had to be to keep up with this young man. The audiences came to see her . . . the first time. But their second and third trips to the Empire were to see Richard Bennett.

Since that time he has gone upward. "Beyond the Horizon," "They Knew What They Wanted," "The Barker," and "Jarnegan" have been vivid things because of him. But Richard Bennett's achievement was the production of Brieux's sensational drama, "Damaged Goods." This was no mere production of a play fraught with the usual hindrances and delays. It was a knockdown, drag-out fight. That play tells the truth about what the squeamish delight to term "a social disease."

"So," said Mr. Bennett, "every church and woman's club fought me and they can fight. I had to use every trick I knew and some I invented to get that play open. If I hadn't had the financial backing of a famous oil family they'd have licked me."

Personally, I doubt that for I never heard of anybody licking Richard Bennett.

"And I have only one devout wish now." He was becoming warmed to his subject. It's the one closest to his heart. "Will somebody please write me a play like 'Damaged Goods,' on the subject of birth control? That's something we are playing ostrich about in this country and I'd like to be the one to smack out of the minds of our people some of the hypocrisy that is so omnipresent. The theater is the place to do it and now the talking pictures.

"THEY'RE the theater now . . . only the picture producers haven't waked up to that fact yet . . . which seems to me to be the answer to what's the matter with pictures.

"Then you'd have birth control and eugenic matters of common knowledge and discussion in every home?"

"We'd see a better race . . . better breeding," he shot back at me and that naturally brought me back to the Bennett breed.

"I suppose you have given your eventual grandchildren some thought?" I suggested.

"I have," he said. He already possesses two. Miss Joan caused him to wear the appellation of "Grandfather" when she was married to John M. Fox and bore little Adrienne Ralston Fox, now three years old, while Constance has a two-year-old son. I asked him if he wanted the family to go on in the theater and when he said he did I wondered just what sort of fathers he would choose so that the strain would be vigorous and imaginative.

"Give me some men in my family like Andrew Jackson and Sam Houston and we would lick the world. What one has to fear for his progeny is the vanity ponderer."

Such vitality added to the Bennett brains and beauty would make a fearful and wonderful combination, especially as these children possess a big dash of Richard Bennett's deadly wit.

After he had outshone Miss Adams in "What Every Woman Knows" he did not play with her any more, but remained most friendly. I suspect he was more friendly with her than she with him. At any rate, he always sent her a telegram on her opening, not forgetting the night she opened at the Empire in Rostand's play "Chantecler." It was a fantastic drama in which all the characters were the animals and fowls of the barn-yard. Miss Adams played the title rôle of Chantecler, which my dictionary informs me is French for rooster.

On that memorable opening night Miss Adams received the following telegram from Richard Bennett.

"Dear Friend: Congratulations. At last you have achieved the ambition of your life. You are your own leading man."

Perhaps the thing that will longest be remembered by this disdainer of feeble customs was his reading of a chapter from the Holy Bible in Texas Guinan's night club. I recalled it—and asked for its effect—He said: "I believe it was the most dramatic few moments I have ever known in my life—when I read the finish—'and the greatest of these is Charity'—the silence was so overwhelming, it seemed, the course of wants had ceased—then the tumult that broke forth convinced me of just another dramatic moment."

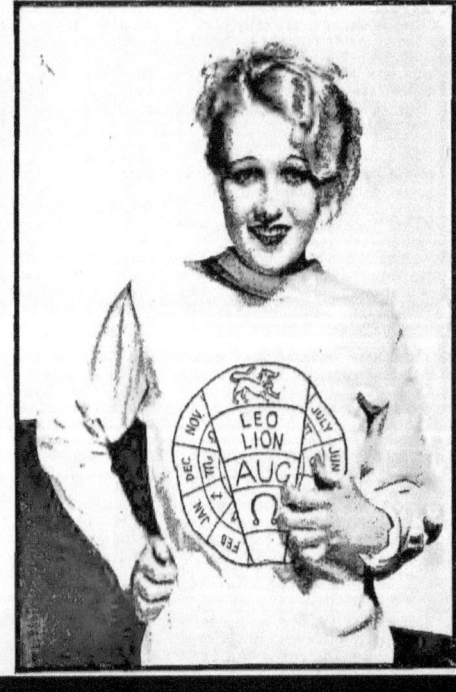

When Evangeline Adams started writing about the motion picture luminaries for NEW MOVIE she launched an astrological vogue in Hollywood. Now the girls out there are wearing their horoscopes on their sweaters. Anita Page is shown all dressed up in the sign of Leo. She was born August 10th.

What They Really WEAR

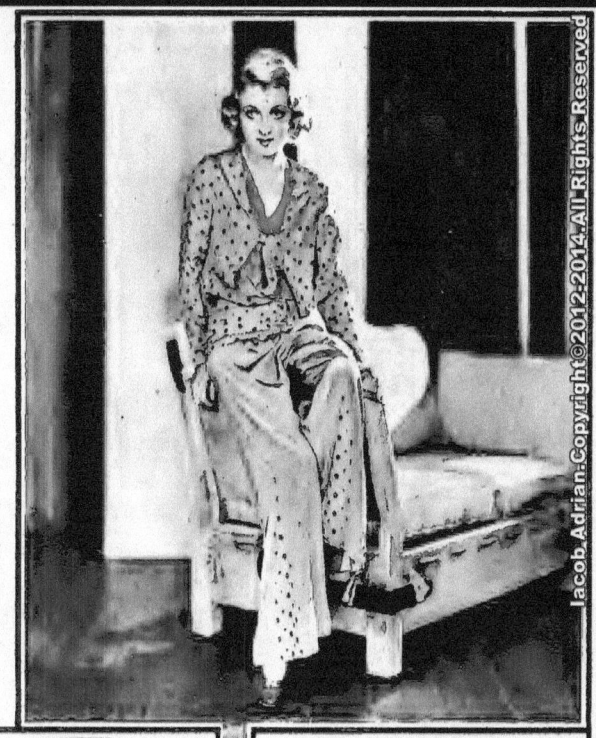

Constance Bennett, shown at the right, wears silk beach pajamas when she isn't before the camera. This is her favorite attire for relaxation. Below, Robert Montgomery, who affects a silk scarf, white flannels, white shoes and a white sweater—all for comfort—when he is on his way to and from the studio. Extreme right, Jack Oakie, in his favorite garb of red and white sweater, black and white striped flannels. Quiet, eh wh—what?

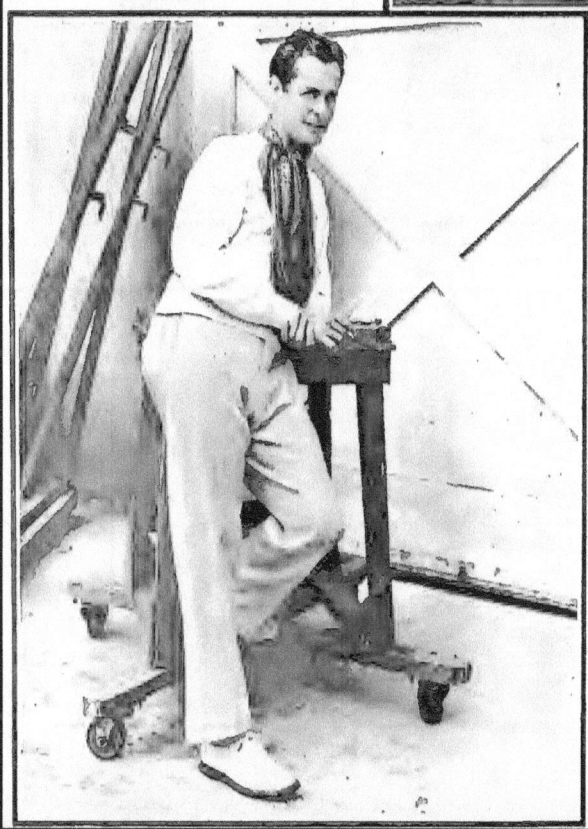

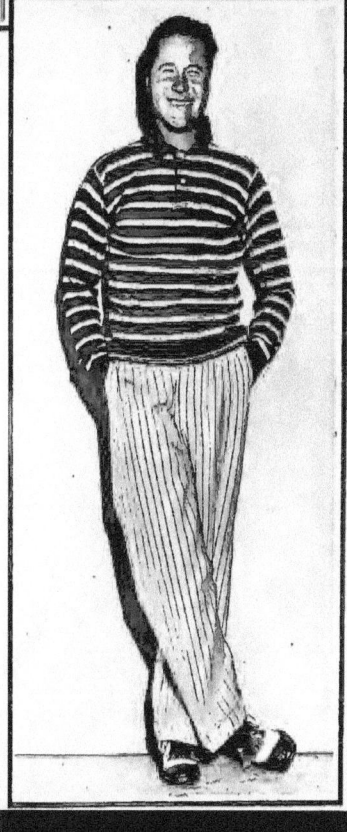

Jacob Adrian Copyright ©2012-2014 All Rights Reserved

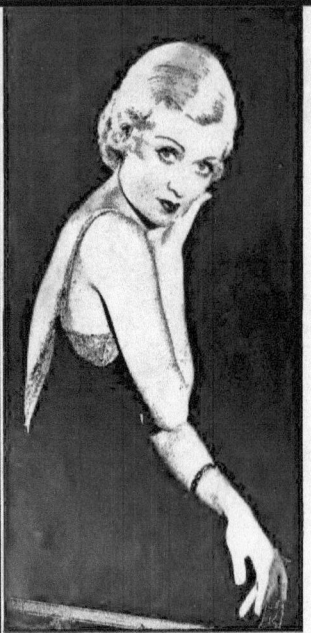

Constance Bennett goes in for custards and desserts—
all she can eat.

Constance Bennett's WEEK'S DIET

This Star's problem isn't how to reduce but how to keep from getting too thin

COUNTING calories is a full-sized job for Constance Bennett. Popovers and caramel custard, Yorkshire pudding and peach mousse—all the dishes that the inclined-to-be-plump must forego are included in her daily diet. Because Constance's problem isn't how to reduce but how to keep from getting too thin. Her menus are those for the girl that wants to fill out the hollows and get away from the string-bean silhouette. Here is her weekly menu:

SUNDAY
Breakfast
Grapefruit   Waffles   Maple Syrup
Buttered Toast
Coffee
Lunch
Persian Melon
Belgian Hare   Wine Sauce
Asparagus Vinaigrette
Caramel Custard   Coffee
Dinner
Cream of Tomato Soup
Roast Leg of Lamb
Mint Sauce
Roast Potatoes   Fresh Garden Peas
Romaine Salad with French Dressing
Chocolate Pudding   Coffee

MONDAY
Breakfast
Sliced Oranges
Sliced Bacon
Popovers   Coffee
Lunch
Fruit Cocktail
Lamb Hash   Mashed Carrots and Turnips
Tomato and Lettuce Salad
Coffee
Dinner
Cream of Pea Soup
Roast Chicken, Dressing
Creamed Potatoes   Corn on Cob
Alligator Pear Salad
Fruit Bowl   Coffee

TUESDAY
Breakfast
Grapefruit Juice   Shirred Eggs
Buttered Toast   Coffee
Lunch
Lamb Chops   Baked Potatoes
Summer Squash   Rice Pudding
Coffee
Dinner
Chicken Soup   Roast Beef   Yorkshire Pudding
Brussels Sprouts   Bowl Salad
Fresh Date Pudding   Coffee

WEDNESDAY
Breakfast
Orange Juice   Poached Egg on Toast
Coffee
Lunch
Irish Stew   Combination Salad
Chocolate Nut Cookies   Coffee
Dinner
Baked Virginia Ham   Wine Sauce
Mashed Potatoes   Red Beets
Spinach Ring
Vanilla Souffle   Coffee

Constance Bennett's Week's Diet

THURSDAY
Breakfast
Sliced Bananas and Cream
Jam Muffins   Coffee
Lunch
Spanish Omelette   Cold Roast Beef
Heads of Lettuce   French Dressing
Floating Island Pudding   Coffee
Dinner
Vegetable Soup
Roast Pork and Apple Sauce
Potatoes Au Gratin
Broccoli with Hollandaise Sauce
Peach Mousse   Coffee

FRIDAY
Breakfast
Stewed Apricots   Buttered Toast
Coffee
Lunch
Cheese Souffle   Vegetable Salad
Apple Tarts   Coffee
Dinner
Creamed Mushrooms on Toast
Baked Swordfish   Tartar Sauce
Spanish Rice
Artichokes Vinaigrette
Lemon Meringue Pie   Coffee

SATURDAY
Breakfast
Baked Apples with Cream
Corn Muffins   Coffee
Lunch
Meat Loaf   Baked Noodles
Stewed Tomatoes
Sliced Peaches   Cookies   Coffee
Dinner
Creamed Asparagus Soup
Roast Duck   Chestnut Dressing
Souffle Potatoes   String Beans
Endive Salad with Sliced Oranges
Vanilla Mousse   Maple Nut Sauce
Coffee

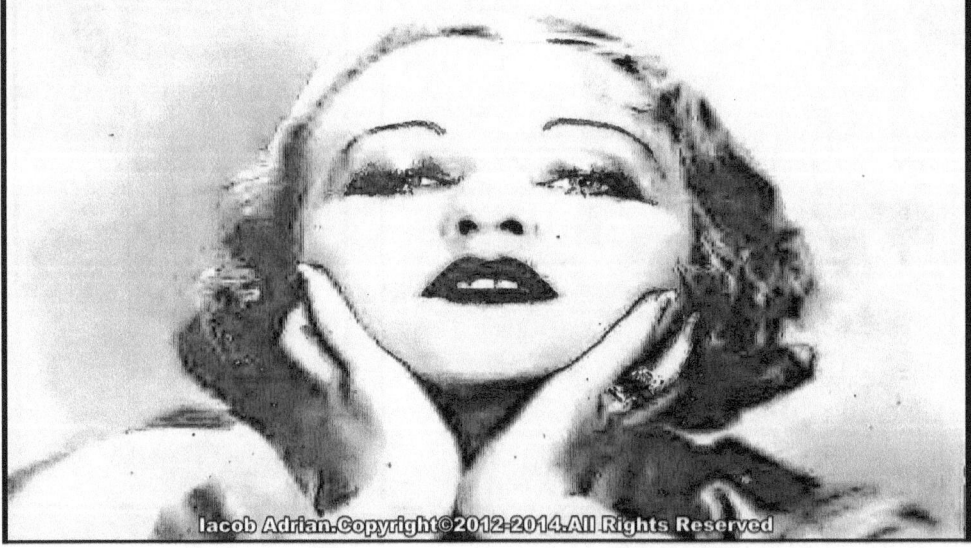

Iacob Adrian.Copyright©2012-2014.All Rights Reserved

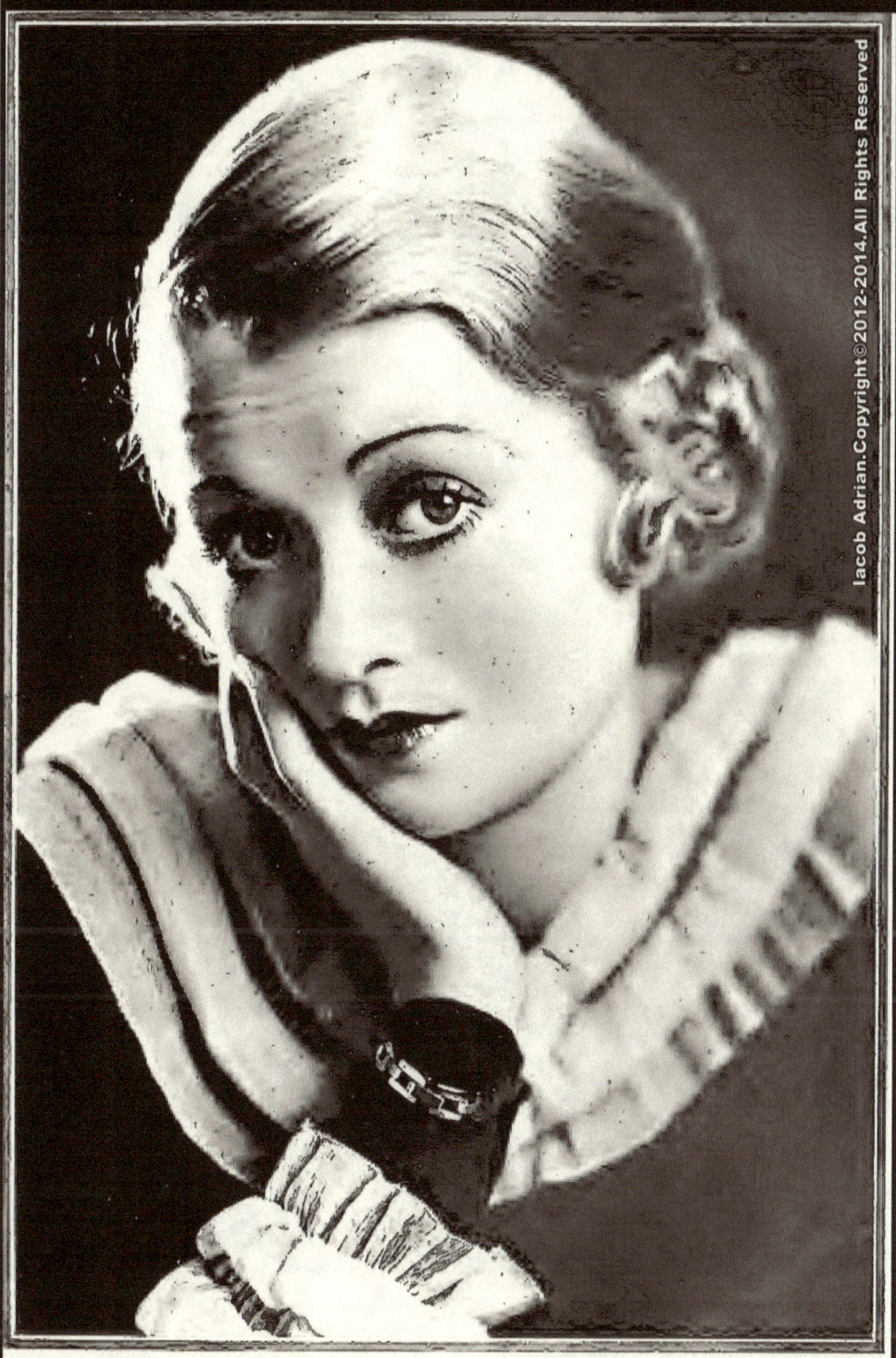

Iacob Adrian.Copyright©2012-2014.All Rights Reserved

CONSTANCE BENNETT

THE STARS TAKE TO TROUSERS

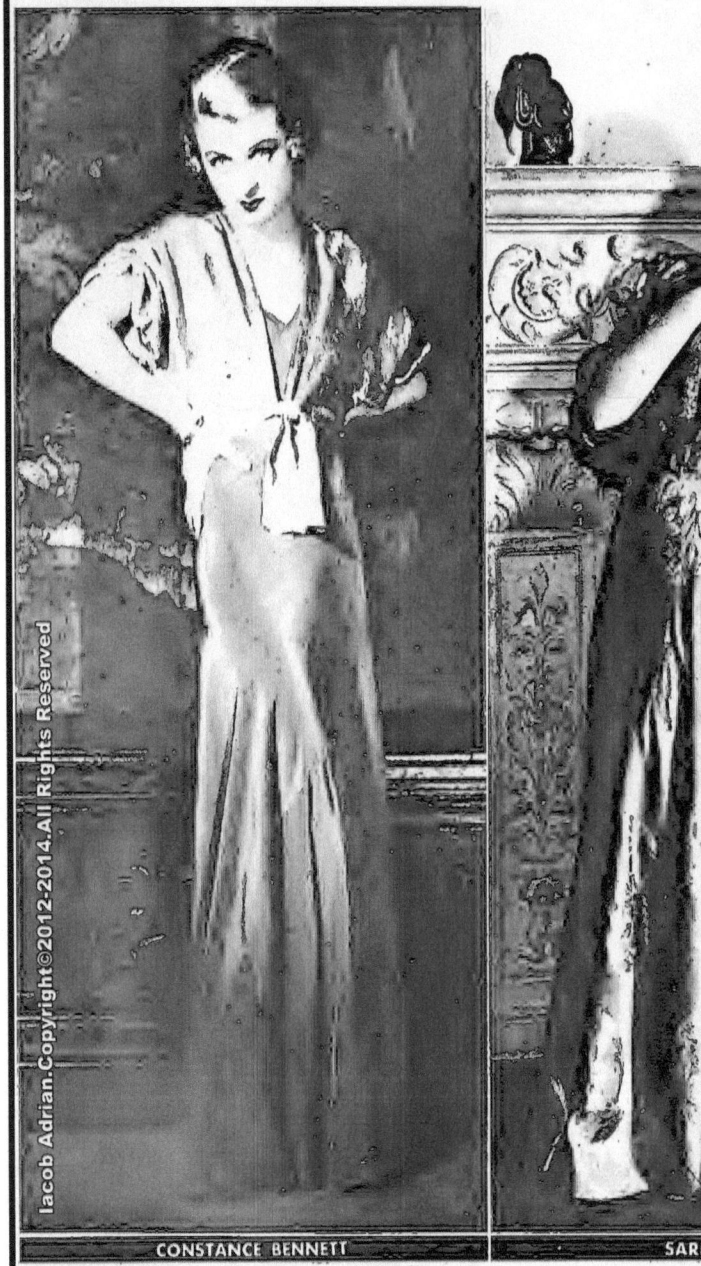

Iacob Adrian.Copyright©2012-2014.All Rights Reserved

Radio Pictures photo

CONSTANCE BENNETT

SARI MARITZA

These blue crêpe pajamas become Connie, as you may notice when you see her wear them in RKO Pathé's "Lady With a Past." The jacket, which is removable, is of pale blue lamé, and the full trousers are of a deeper shade of crêpe.

Formal dinner pajamas of blue, too. Twilight blue taffeta this time, embossed with a motif worked in silver thread. The trousers are hardly discernible as such, and a tiny removable cape covers the shoulders and the low décolletage.

Hollywood's Most
Misunderstood Girl

Iacob Adrian Copyright©2012-2014 All Rights Reserved

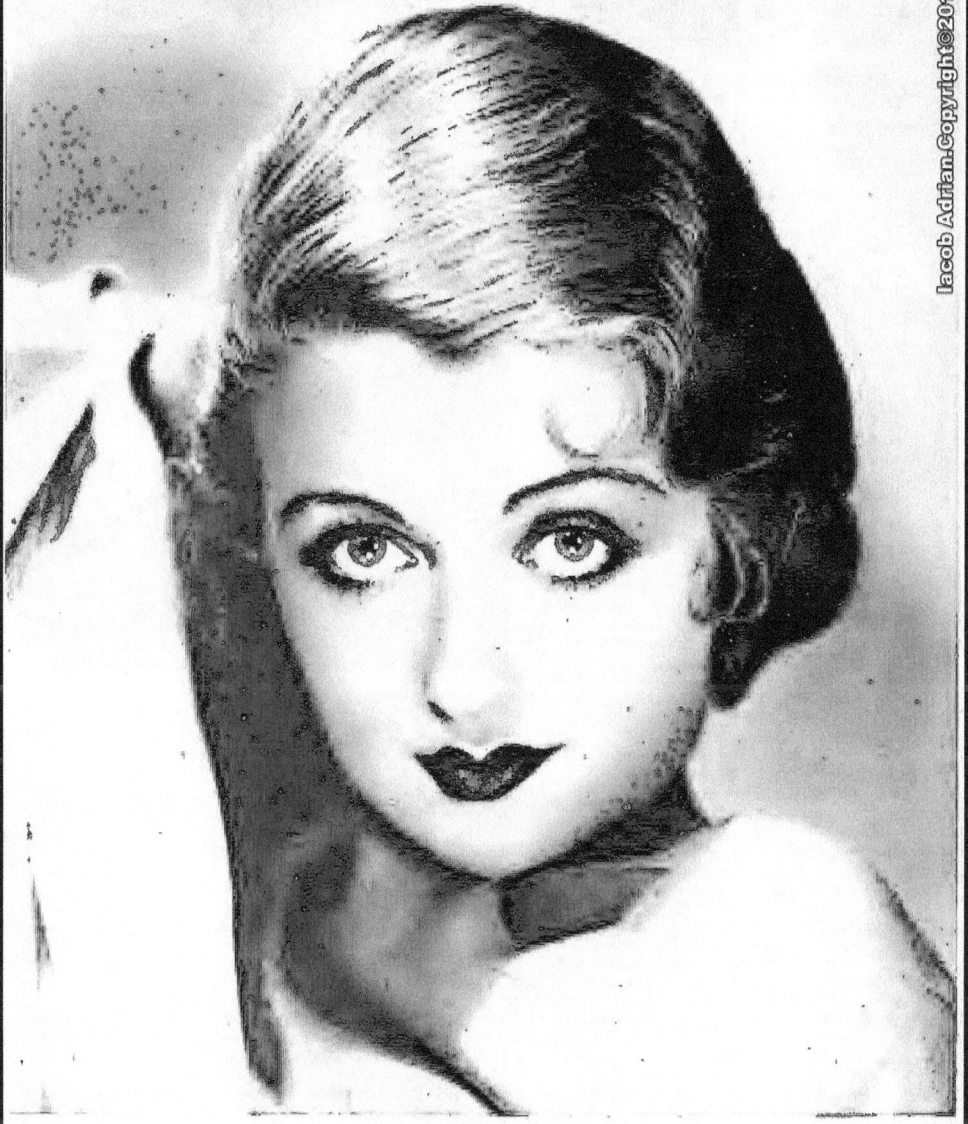

"Connie goes right on standing on the firing line. In the face of calumny, malice
and dastardly invention, she refuses to lower her colors."

Iacob.Adrian.Copyright©2012-2014.All Rights Reserved

At last!—the truth about

Constance Bennett—as only

ADELA ROGERS ST. JOHNS

can write it

MANY prices are paid for fame. Constance Bennett has paid one of the highest.

They've called her high hat. They've headlined the idea that she is unpopular in Hollywood. They've painted her as a temperamental egotist, always demanding her own way and careless of those crushed beneath her chariot wheels. Tales about her are legion —about the enormous salary she gets, the unheard of amount she wastes on clothes, the arrogance she displays in the studio, her disregard for the rights of other women.

Connie goes right on standing on the firing line. In the face of calumny, malice and dastardly invention, she refuses to lower her colors.

It just happens that she isn't any of these things. She is a gallant lady with too much guts for her own good and too much integrity for the racket she's in. And that's the truth if I starve for it.

The terrific injustice done Connie didn't worry me much, because I thought she didn't care. I used to misunderstand her myself. But, because we have become friends, I found out that she does care and that beneath the armor of her indifference she carries a deep and bitter hurt.

The most misunderstood girl in Hollywood! And be hanged to everybody if she's going to explain herself!

THERE you have Connie. A woman who meets men on their own ground, who asks no favors, who offers no alibis. With wise eyes that are sometimes sad, she watches the game of star-baiting go on, and knows that she is being pilloried because she says what she thinks, minds her own business and fights her own battles. But she hasn't the Nordic isolation of Garbo, and it hurts.

Humble as to her great success, loyal to, and gentle with her friends, a really square guy with everybody who works for her, she is prouder than Satan in the face of injustice and misunderstanding. Proud—much too proud. Making no concessions and no compromises with life. There she is—going about her own affairs, doing her work, living her life. If people are unkind enough to misjudge her, to resent her demand for privacy, she will not stoop to ask for understanding.

Never a woman of great strength, privacy is an utter necessity to her. Without those hours alone, she couldn't carry on. Without a certain amount of quiet, she wouldn't be able to make pictures. But she never mentions that and so they call her high hat.

It is the general impression that Connie is untouched by the fantastic stories which have been spread broadcast.

The way I came to find out how deeply wounded she has been by it all is this:

One bright spring morning somebody called "Yoohoo" under the window of my work-room at Malibu. Always delighted with an excuse to abandon my labors, I went to the window. A slim, blonde girl in a plain bathing suit and a small towheaded boy in infini-

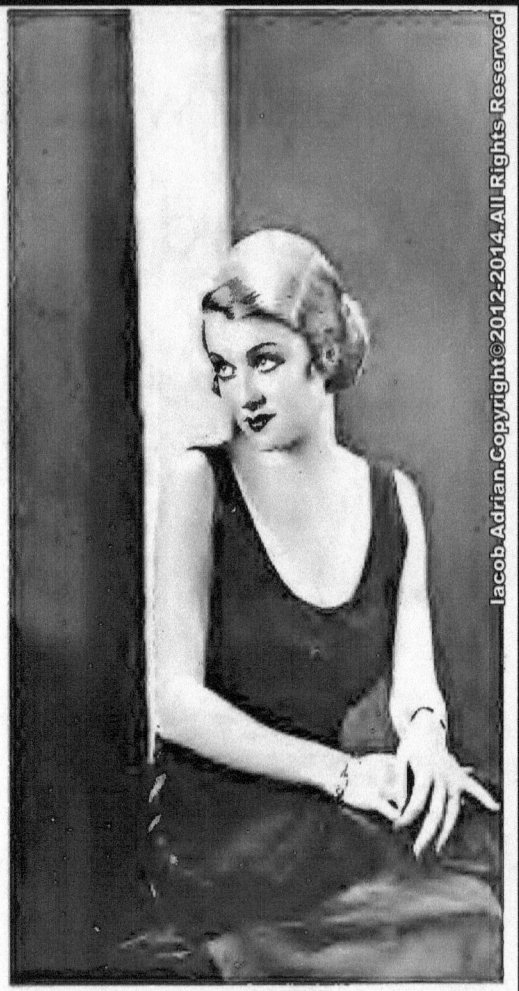

Constance Bennett—"A woman who meets men on their own ground, who asks no favors, who offers no alibis. With wise eyes that are sometimes sad, she watches the game."

tesimal trunks stood there, gazing up. The beach was silvery with sunshine. The blue water danced and sparkled.

"Come on down and play with us," called Connie Bennett. "I've got a day off and Peter wants to see Dicky."

I unearthed my three-year-old son from the backyard; where he was doing all right with a hammer, and the four of us went adventuring. While the two kids dug strange looking sea animals from the rocks, and fell in and out of the Pacific with yelps of glee, Connie and I sat on the sand and talked.

It was then I discovered that Constance Bennett carries a torch. Not for any man. But for the fans who should love her and who have been lied to about her.

"BUT what can you do?" said Connie, letting the sand run through her fingers and gazing absently at the small boy she adopted. "You can't go around squawking and squealing, can you? When somebody comes around and asks you why you aren't popular, you can't become tearful. If people want to know about things that are strictly your

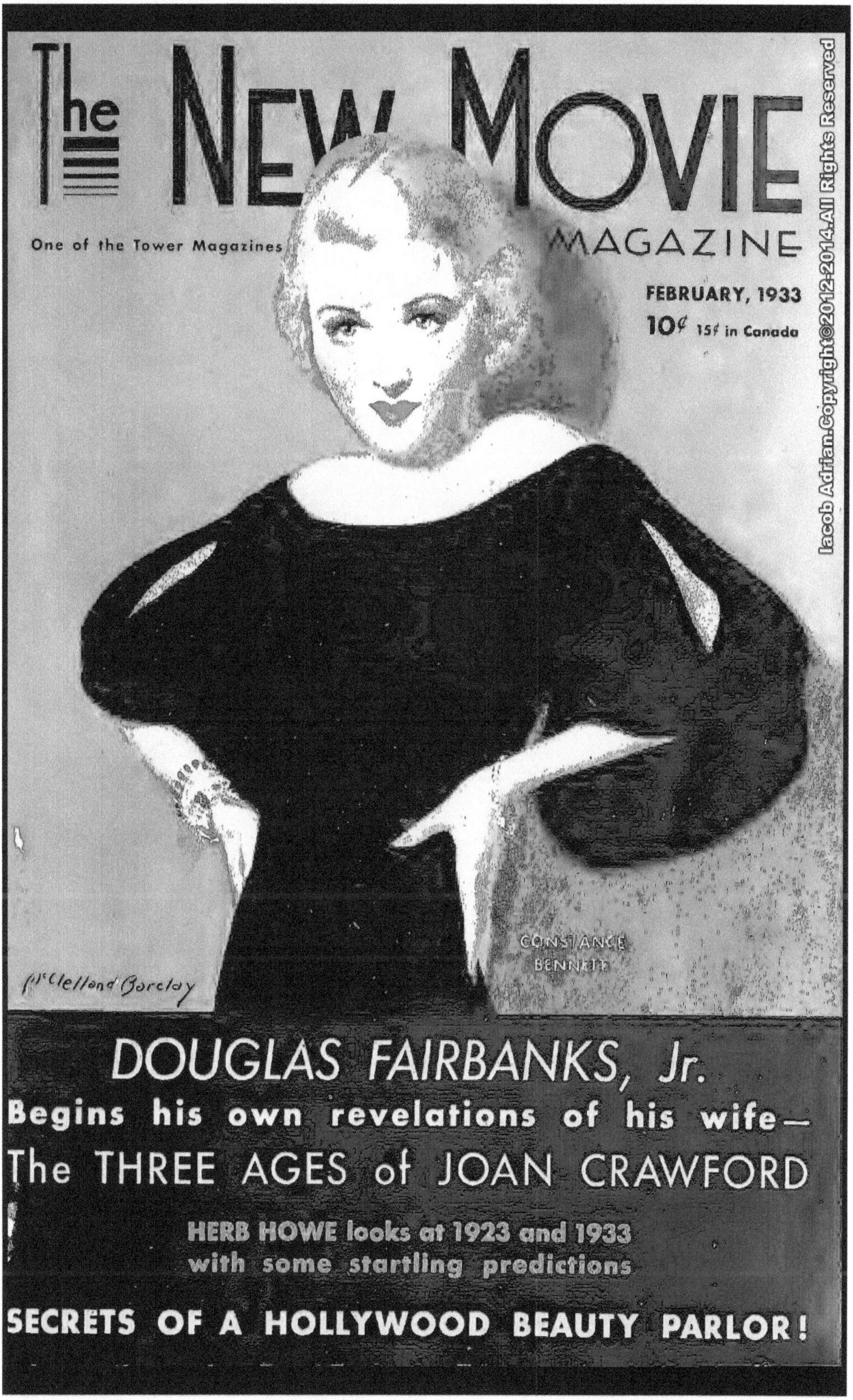

The NEW MOVIE MAGAZINE

One of the Tower Magazines

FEBRUARY, 1933

10¢ 15¢ in Canada

Iacob Adrian Copyright©2012-2014 All Rights Reserved

McClelland Barclay

CONSTANCE BENNETT

DOUGLAS FAIRBANKS, Jr.
Begins his own revelations of his wife—
The THREE AGES of JOAN CRAWFORD

HERB HOWE looks at 1923 and 1933 with some startling predictions

SECRETS OF A HOLLYWOOD BEAUTY PARLOR!

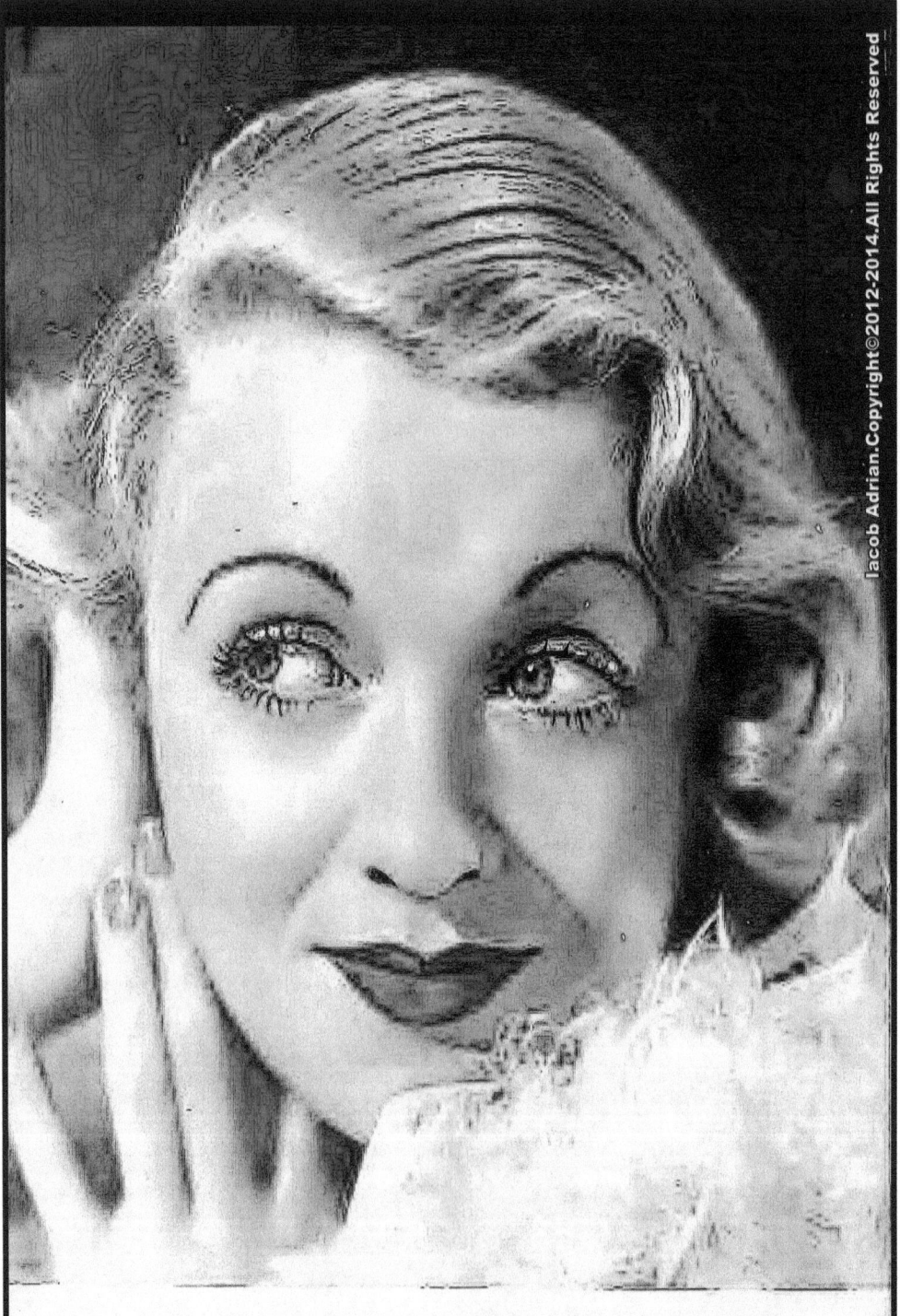

Iacob Adrian.Copyright©2012-2014.All Rights Reserved

Finishing her latest, "Bed of Roses," Connie Bennett has hied
herself to the United Artists to appear in Darryl Zannuck's Twentieth
Century pictures, while the Marquis is off in remote places supervis-
ing Bennett Productions, Inc. What next for Connie?

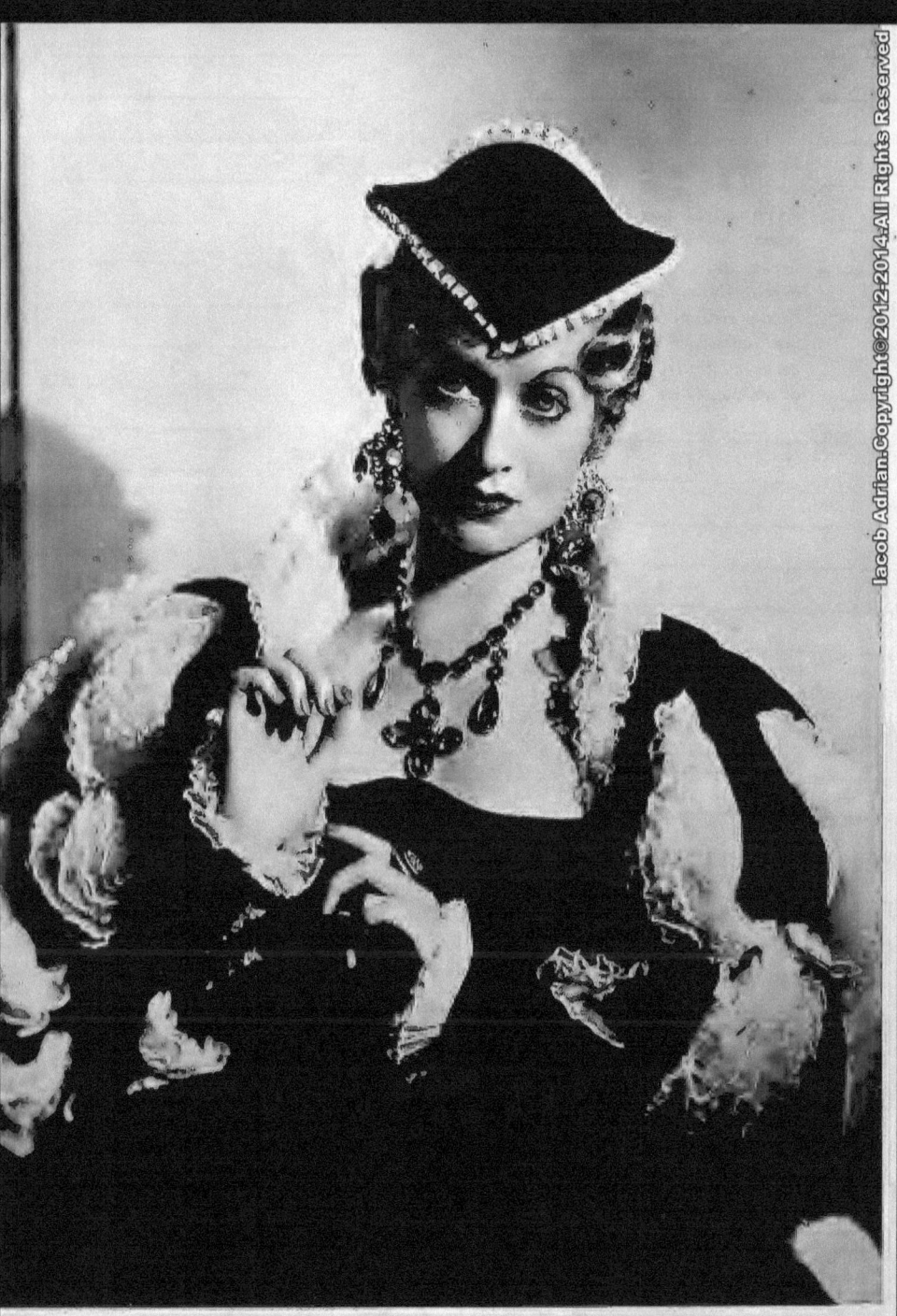

Iacob Adrian Copyright©2012-2014 All Rights Reserved

CONSTANCE BENNETT—Costumed thus for her part in 20th Century's "The Affairs of Cellini," Constance Bennett causes one to wonder why Cellini's loves were plural. No more fascinating lady could have been found in all medieval Italy. In "Moulin Rouge" she gave you two diverse personalities. Here is a third, even more provocative.

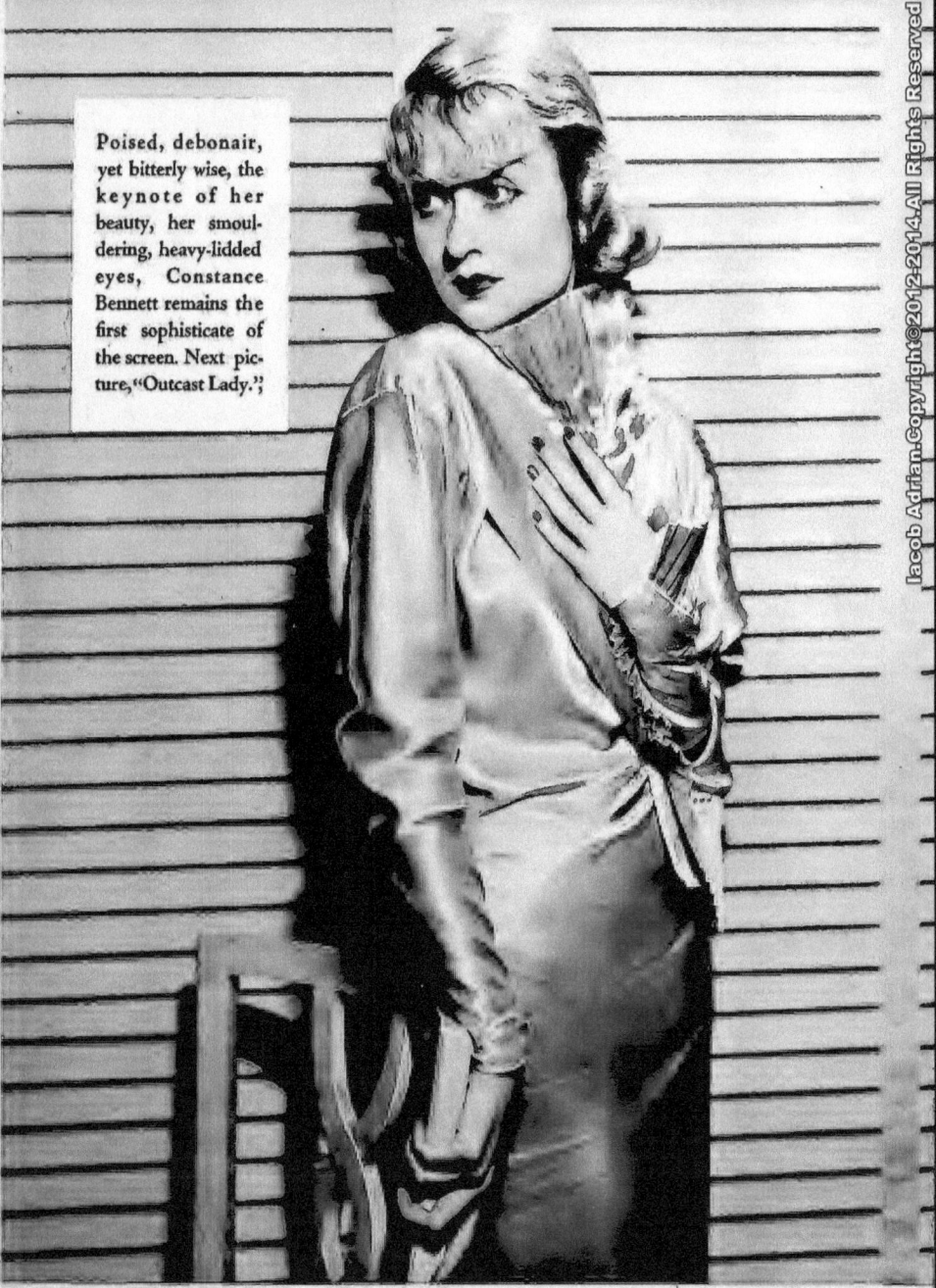

Poised, debonair, yet bitterly wise, the keynote of her beauty, her smouldering, heavy-lidded eyes, Constance Bennett remains the first sophisticate of the screen. Next picture, "Outcast Lady.";

Iacob Adrian Copyright©2012-2014.All Rights Reserved

THE NEW MOVIE MAGAZINE'S

GALLERY of STARS

Bibliographic sources :

Hollywood (1934-1943)
Publisher: Hollywood Magazine, inc. ; Fawcett Publications, inc.

The New Movie Magazine (1929-1935)
Publisher: Tower Magazines, inc.

This documentary study use,
combined in various proportions,
elements from the following categories,
forms and subsets :
- fair use
- documentary
- documentary photography
- feature
- journalism
- arts journalism
- visual journalism
- photojournalism
- celebrity photography
in order to :
- employ material as the object of cultural critique ,
- quote to illustrate an argument or point ,
- use material in historical sequence,
providing independent opinion,
using photos, press articles, advertisements,
opinions of fans etc. ...

Copyright©2012-2014 Iacob Adrian
All Rights Reserved.

www.ingramcontent.com/pod-product-compliance
Lightning Source LLC
Chambersburg PA
CBHW021026180526
45163CB00005B/2143